THE
Archive Photographs
SERIES

ELY, CAERAU
AND MICHAELSTON-SUPER-ELY

Canterbury Tales by Chaucer

but →

ELY ALES
BY CHOICE

THE BREWERY · ELY · CARDIFF

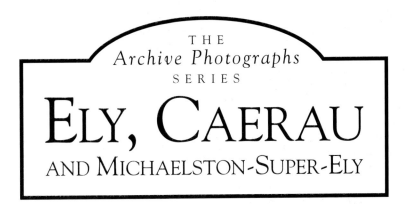

THE
Archive Photographs
SERIES

ELY, CAERAU
AND MICHAELSTON-SUPER-ELY

Compiled by
Nigel Billingham and Stephen K. Jones

CHALFORD

First published 1996
Copyright © Nigel Billingham and Stephen K. Jones, 1996

The Chalford Publishing Company
St Mary's Mill, Chalford,
Stroud, Gloucestershire, GL6 8NX

ISBN 0 7524 0656 6

Typesetting and origination by
The Chalford Publishing Company
Printed in Great Britain by
Redwood Books, Trowbridge

Also published in the *Archive Photographs* series:

Canton (Bryan Jones)
Cardiff City Football Club, 1899-1947 (Richard Shepherd)
Dinas Powys, St Andrews Major and Michaelston-le-Pit (Chrystal Tilney)
Grangetown (Barbara Jones)
Llandaff (The Llandaff Society)
Roath, Splott and Adamsdown (Jeff Childs)

Front cover illustration:
Ely Brewery workers, c. 1915.

Cowbridge Road. Although the road was part of the main highway from Cardiff to West Wales it presented a much calmer and less hurried scene some eighty years ago.

Contents

Revd Bob Morgan.

Foreword

Ely has to be lived in to be truly appreciated. I will always value serving thirty-four years as the parish priest of the Church of Resurrection and twenty of those years as a Cardiff City and a South Glamorgan Councillor. My wife Elaine, of course, joined me and served Ely very efficiently.

From the days of the old Res. discos in the 1960s, Ely has built up a network of local organisations such as playgroups for pre-school children, a day centre for the elderly, a major family centre, 'Healthy Wealthy and Wise' for the over 50s, two credit unions, Cardiff's first leisure centre for our young sports enthusiasts, with the culmination every year in the grand Ely Carnival and Festival attracting up to 20,000 people. The area is alive with life interest groups, and it was this opportunity to celebrate life in all its fullness that kept me and my family in Ely for the whole of my family life. God has been very good to us.

Nigel Billingham and Steve Jones are household names in Ely and great contributors to its vibrant life. They have worked hard to record the marvellous people and events which make us proud to be Ely. Ely has come of age, we have a history. I do recommend that every family buys a copy and hands it down to their children. Tell them 'these are the golden years of Ely and we were there'.

Canon Bob Morgan OBE
County Councillor (1973-1993)
City Councillor (1973-1981)
Leader, South Glamorgan County Council (1981-1986)
Chairman, South Glamorgan County Council (1991)

Preface

The area commonly referred to as Ely today was originally composed of three parishes: Ely (which technically was not a parish in its own right but a hamlet of the larger Llandaff parish) Caerau, Michaelston-super-Ely, and also part of the St Fagans parish. Their boundaries were well defined but the westward expansion of Cardiff in the 1920s was to absorb and blur the former rural communities. In 1922 the city boundary was extended to include the parishes of Llandaff (including Ely), Caerau, Michaelston-super-Ely and the southern part of St Fagans. The building of the City Council estates then began and the whole area has grown into one of the most densely populated suburbs of Cardiff.

As the title indicates, *The Archive Photographs Series* sets out to present the history of an area as recorded through the camera lens. With this in mind it has not been possible, and indeed it may not be desirable in a work of this nature, to fully outline the rich and varied history of the area. However, we hope that the images illustrated will convey the variety of life in an area that, to quote Revd Bob Morgan, 'has come of age' and give readers a glimpse into a now lost rural landscape, the effect of industrialisation and the making of a community.

Nigel Billingham
(Project Leader at Barnardos Ely Community Shop, 1975-89)
Stephen K. Jones
(Chairman of Ely Archives Project, 1986-88, and Ely resident for over forty years)

Caerau's Iron Age hill-fort, 1984. The earth ramparts of the main enclosure can be clearly seen in this recent photograph.

One

Early History
and the Church

A great diversity of history can be found in the Ely area as it has been inhabited since prehistoric times. Neolithic tribes colonised the area and the huge tombs of their leaders still exist at Tinkerswood and St Lythans. Various objects dating back to 3000 BC have been uncovered in Ely, such as a flint axe-head found near Frank Road, and a flint chisel found at the former Caerau Brickworks. The first Celts landed at the mouth of the River Ely, where rare stone razors dating from the seventh century BC have been found. As the Roman Empire expanded across Europe, the Celtic people were pushed westwards, some finally settling in the Ely area. Continual fighting between tribes made protection from enemies essential so large hillforts were constructed of which the camp at Caerau is an impressive example.

The River Ely rises in the hills behind Gilfach Goch, flowing down through Tonyrefail, Pontyclun, Peterston-super-Ely, winding through St Fagans and Ely to enter the sea between Penarth and Cardiff. The river used to silt up in the Ely Bridge area and therefore provided a convenient fording point for travellers heading westwards. The current main road through Ely – Cowbridge Road West – was a prehistoric trackway on which a Roman military road was constructed from Gloucester to Neath for the purpose of facilitating operations against the many tribes of south Wales. Sextus Julius Frontinus, the constructor of the highway had been sent to Britain in AD 75 as a provincial governor; the road was named 'Via Julia Maritima' after him. The crossing at Ely was known as Pont Lai or Eley. The road later became known as the Portway and was referred to as such up to the nineteenth century.

In 1894, the remains of a Romano-British villa and foundry were discovered on the site of Ely Racecourse. The villa stood on a road made of pebble stones, which led straight to Ely Bridge. Many household articles were found, including silver, bronze, and lead coins, jewellery, pottery jars, and several bones. The foundry, which was a military forge, had a hearth which used mainly coal from a seam at Pentyrch. Manganese ore from Spain was also discovered, and the Cardiff Naturalists Society reported in 1894 that 'it is certain that manganese ore was used in the manufacture of steel at Sheffield long before… any of the modern steel makers… and it is quite possible that the secret may have come down from the remote period when the Roman works at Ely was working, as trade secrets were always strictly guarded'.

THE HAMLET OF ELY UP TO THE MIDDLE AGES

At the time of the Norman invasion of Glamorgan in the 1080s, Ely was a tiny hamlet clustered round the river crossing. Ely was in the lordship of the bishop of Llandaff, whose estate included the village of Canton, as well as the hamlets of Caerau, Fairwater, Llandaff North and Gabalfa. The bishop owned a mill with land and a fishery at Ely given to him as a gift in 1126. The marshland and forest bordering the River Ely remained undeveloped throughout the Middle Ages, although the river crossing remained an important one, as it had been for centuries. The hamlet of Ely remained small and little documented. From the fourteenth century there were tithe barns at Ely, Caerau and Fairwater for the collection of tithes (taxes paid to the Church). Llandaff parish records show that these barns were still in use in the eighteenth century.

DEVELOPMENT OF THE MAIN ROAD

The main road running through the hamlet of Ely remained the most important route between West Wales and Llandaff. John Leland writing between 1539 and 1545 refers to Ely Bridge being of stone construction and having two arches. In 1697, the roads were still cart tracks and their maintenance costs fell upon the parish; at this time the parish was reported for failing to repair the road at Ely Pool which was described as in a 'perilous condition'.

Up until the 1750s, people only travelled by foot or horseback and the condition of the poorly maintained roads left much to be desired, making even short journeys a dangerous and time-consuming undertaking. By 1784, mail coaches were passing through Ely from Cardiff on their way to Cowbridge and Milford Haven. Coaches demanded a higher standard of road repair and when the law made it legal for tolls to be charged for their upkeep, turnpike roads became widespread. A turnpike house stood on the main road approximately half way between Caerau Lane and Amroth Road. It collected tolls until 1889 and was demolished around 1930. Three cast-iron milestones erected by the Turnpike Trust can still be seen today at mile intervals along Cowbridge Road West.

In 1792, following a report on the state of roads and bridges throughout South Wales, it was decided to improve the ten-foot wide Ely Bridge, by extending the arches north and south at a cost of £4 17s 3d. An additional £97 was allocated for breaking stones and gravelling 1,940 yards of road. The road was widened many times using locally quarried stone. During one such scheme of road widening at the turn of the century the bones of an unknown 'traveller' were unearthed near the Dusty Forge inn (then called Efail y Dwst).

Romano-British villa site, Ely Racecourse, 1984. The land here was farmed by George Thomas of Ely Farm. Prior to its excavation, the ancient site was, in common with popular belief, thought to be that of a monastery.

ST MARY'S CHURCH

St Mary's church, Caerau is the oldest stone structure in the parish but now stands isolated and derelict on a hilltop within the main enclosure of an Iron Age hill-fort. An earlier church stood just to the north of the Norman building, with traces still visible in 1913. This first church was probably dedicated to St Gweirydd ab Brochfael (ruler of Morgannwg around AD 900). Like most Celtic churches, it would have been of timber construction; the Normans constructed a stone building around 1260. The new church was valued at £4 (under the deanery of Newport) in 1291. Enlarged over the years, it was the subject of a Protestant outburst during the reign of Edward VI (1547-1553) when the rood-loft was ripped out and the internal wall murals were destroyed. Major restoration was carried out from 1881 to 1889 largely at the expense of Lieut. Col. E.S. Hill CB (later Sir Edward Hill MP) of 'Rookwood', Llandaff, a major landowner in Caerau, and the Marquess of Bute. By 1957, however, St Mary's was badly vandalised, deconsecrated and closed down, but in 1959 the Revd Victor Jones, with many helpers, began the rebuilding, which was completed in 1961 and followed by a service of consecration. A vestry was added at this time. In the early 1970s, however, the church was deconsecrated for the second time.

Up until 1869, Ely's parish church was Llandaff Cathedral, but then the village was transferred to the living of St Mary's, Caerau. The baptismal register shows the first baptism with a vicar, the Revd E. John, taking place in November 1869. Previous baptisms, which only numbered a few each year, were made by an officiating minister named as curate of Caerau. All these births were children from the Caerau district, but, thereafter, Ely births were registered as well, frequently from a thatched cottage in Mill Road (where Grover's Terrace was subsequently built), which had been used for a weekly service before 1869, and continued until the opening of St David's in 1871.

Opposite: The castle and the church, 1984. Overlooked by the now ruined parish church of Caerau, St Mary's, is an oval ringwork believed to be a medieval castle site. Current opinion suggests that it was constructed in the twelfth century for the bishop of Llandaff. It is from this feature that the name Caerau (Welsh for 'walls' or 'forts') is derived.

11

St Mary's church, *c.* 1940. The church stands on a hill overlooking Caerau which the Ely Link Road (A 432) skirts to the north. In the churchyard there was a magnificent yew tree, said to be 2,000 years old. On 6 July 1937 the tree was found burning by Miss Macbride of Ivy Cottage, Caerau. Even then the church was suffering vandalism.

St Michael's church, in the parish of Michaelston-super-Ely, stands well-maintained in its restored condition. In the Norman style with saddleback-roof west towers, it dates from about the late twelfth century and some of the original herring-bone masonry work can be seen in the base of the north wall. The chancel probably soon followed, with the tower and porch built late in the fourteenth century. The small transept was added last, in the sixteenth century. St Michael's major restoration in 1863-4 by David Vaughan has been much criticised for its alterations and additions.

Two
The Rural Parishes

Michaelston-super-Ely, although like Caerau a parish in its own right, was in the Dinas Powis Hundred (Ely and Caerau being part of the Kibbor or Cardiff Hundred). It also differed ecclesiastically in that its parish church of St Michael's appears never to have been a possession of Llandaff Cathedral nor appropriated to any abbey or priory. St Michael's origins lie in the manorial system imposed by the Normans following their subjugation of Glamorgan. In 1254, its value was assessed at 40 shillings in the Norwich Taxation. As a manor, Michaelston-super-Ely formed part of the Lordship of Glamorgan which was granted to Sir William Herbert (1st Earl of Pembroke) in 1550. Over the years ownership passed through a succession of lords of the manor, including, from 1688 to 1702, John Baron Jefferies, son of the infamous hanging judge. For the last two hundred years the title of Lord of the Manor of Michaelston-Super-Ely has remained with the Traherne family. At 299 acres, it was the smallest rural parish in Glamorgan.

The Caerau parish covered 746 acres ranging from Culverhouse to Ely Hospital and back as far as Ballas and Penylan farms. Within the parish was the manor of Sweldon. Caerau Lane was the main parish road, with Caerau village located roughly between the Highfields public house and the bottom of St Mary's Hill. This village 'core' can still be discerned today. Michaelston-super-Ely, in contrast, was considered to be a decayed village over two hundred years ago and very little remains today. In 1837 the parochial rates of Caerau amounted to £52, of which £30 was designated for the relief of the poor. The parish's population was then 77, rising by 1861 to 131. Of these, 78 were born in Glamorganshire and 53 elsewhere, of which 28 came from Ireland. The majority of the inhabitants were labourers, although Caerau did have one shepherd, a woodcutter and a dressmaker. The main farms in the village at that time were Caerau and Ty Newydd. Caerau farmhouse is now the Highfields public house. Ty Newydd farmhouse also remains and can be seen on Heol Trelai next to the 'Hill Dip' shop. By 1915, the parish population was 220, with two brickworks, a post office at Saintwell, a pub – The Caerau Arms – and various smallholdings. Up until 1939, the village remained essentially rural, but RAF Llandaff, a barrage-balloon site, was built on Caerau Lane and council houses were planned and built after the war. House building has continued to this day, with the recent development on the site of Sweldon Farm.

Yr hen Shon Goch o'r Caerau
A aeth i foddi'r gath
Mewn cwd o ganfas newydd,
Nad oedd e' ronyn gwa'th
Y cwd aeth gyda'r afon,
A'r gath a ddaeth i'r lan;
O'r hen Shon Goch o'r Caerau,
Shwd buost ti mor wan!

The Old John Goch of Caerau
He went to drown the cat
In a new bag of canvas,
By the riverside he sat.
The bag went down the river,
The cat crawled to the shore;
O, Old John Goch of Caerau,
You look so very sore!

(Old rhyme)

Cottage in Ely, early 1900s. This stood in Mill Road and was demolished in 1913. Standing in front are Mr Bill (left), John Lloyd and Jane Saunders. At the beginning of the 1800s, Ely had a population of about 180 (the total population of Llandaff parish in 1801 was 860). The village centre consisted of the 'Great House' with other houses clustered around Mill Road and the Bridge. Mill Road was only a lane leading to the corn mill at Cartwright Lane or Birdies Lane as it is known locally. Other lanes led to Ely Farm, Caerau and St Fagans. The people fetched water either from the river or a couple of wells in the village.

Cottage, early 1900s. Now demolished, it was situated on Ely Road, opposite the end of Windway Road.

Culverhouse Farm, c. 1906. Named after the dovecote (or culverhouse) that once provided fresh meat in the form of doves and pigeons, the farm is of pre-1765 origin and stood to the west of Michaelston Road. It was demolished in the early 1960s, to make way for the Michaelston estate. The name survives in the nearby public house – The Culverhouse Cross.

Farmhouse on Ely Common, 29 December 1913. This, like Pwll Coch Farm, was displaced by the laying-out of streets west of Victoria Park.

Ely Farm, 1930s. George Thomas was the most famous resident of the farm, taking up occupation in 1843. The Thomas family lived in the farm from 1832 until 1930 when it passed to the Davies family. Still used as a base for Ely Farm Dairies, it was rebuilt as a Victorian model farmhouse and can still be seen at the end of Dyfrig Road [see page 30].

Ely Farm milk bottle. This red label bottle held two pints.

16

Haymaking with pike in the Western Cemetery fields. Almost opposite the current main entrance to the cemetery stands a row of terraced cottages. Next to The Culverhouse Cross public house, at the end of the terrace, the old Caerau Arms (Hotel) can still be seen. It is first mentioned specifically in a St Mary's church register from 1873 when a June Davies then living at the pub married William Kent, who later became the landlord. The Caerau Arms closed in the late 1930s when The Culverhouse Cross was built.

Green Farm, photographed on 21 March 1952. By 1920, Green Farm and Culverhouse Farm had been merged as one unit and was being farmed by Harry Thorn. It was subsequently purchased by the Cardiff Corporation in a derelict state for £31,339 and operated as a pig farm. During the Second World War parts of the farm were used to store cinema films shown throughout South Wales and the West Country. It was not by enemy action, however, that a fire broke out on 17 April 1945 destroying 50 tons of cinema film. The building is used today as a hostel.

Aerial view of Sweldon Farm, Caerau Lane (Sweldon Hill), c. 1970. Sweldon was a manor belonging to a cadet branch of the Mathew family for many generations. The manor house, now lost, stood opposite the later farmhouse (records of which date from the 1600s).

THE DIARIST WILLIAM THOMAS (1727-1795) has left a revealing insight into life in a local community in the eighteenth century. Born the eldest child of William and Elizabeth Thomas of Michaelston-super-Ely, he could claim descent from the Mathew family, his mother belonging to one of the branches of that family. What form of education he received is uncertain, but he was to hold several posts such as schoolmaster, Clerk to the Commissioners of Taxes for the Hundred of Dinas Powis and land surveyor. His personal observations, recorded in his diary, give a rare account of rural life in Glamorgan during the latter half of the eighteenth century. Roy Denning has recently abridged and edited the surviving manuscript (covering the years 1762-1795), and this published version provides a unique source of information on the lives of ordinary people in a south-east corner of Glamorgan. For example, on 3 June 1765, Thomas notes the progress on the turnpike and some work he was involved with in measuring land taken for its construction: 'The work goes on with speed, and from 80 to 100 on work here and there from Cardiff to Cowbridge'.

An entry the following month (21 July 1766) relates the story of the murder by Philip Evan of Eley of his wife Jane Griffith, alias Evan 'being he was drunk and was Informed that she was likewise... And his wife was a very drunken one, selling the cheese and butter as soon as made, and her clothes, and all she could come to it, for ale. She was drunk the Night before as the report runs, the morning after she was murdered, seven Quarts of ale'. On 31 July the entry states: 'A fair in Eley on the Household stuff and chattels of Philip Evan, now in Jail for murdering his wife'. Philip Evan was, however, cleared of murder at the Cardiff Sessions on 5 August 1766.

Although William Thomas comments disapprovingly on drunkenness in the diary, it was the custom for parish officers to drink on the parish expense when on official business and one of the latter entries (1792) concerns his own experience: 'After ten weeks sore leg, in that, after I passed Cayra's Accompts the Evening of the 25th of May last, I came by Dusty Forge and Drank the share of four pints of ale, but had Drank some before at Cayra and at that could not go away, but lost my senses. And either by slumbering too near the fire, or that hot water came or cast on me, my leg swollen and the skin slipt away that I had great wounds upon it and was in a pityful condition for the time before mentioned'!

Sweldon Farm wedding around 1910. The Emersons were the last family to farm Sweldon with William Emerson taking up occupation on 25 April 1875. Active in Saintwell chapel and political circles, he was a staunch liberal and Sweldon was visited by Lloyd George on one occasion.

Sweldon Farm, 1979. The farm was slowly encroached by housing and school development with Cyntwell High School (now Mary Immaculate Roman Catholic School) taking up land that used to be the farm's market garden. Mrs Emerson, the wife of William Emerson's grandson, decided enough was enough in 1979 and soon afterwards the farm was demolished. New housing development was built on the site with the names Sweldon Close and Farmhouse Way recalling a vanished past.

The David family at Penylan Farm, c. 1920. Still farmed by the Davids today, Penylan Farm, on the border of Caerau and Michaelston-le-Pit parishes, was recorded in the 1861 census as a farm of 74 acres.

Goods on View Morning of Sale.
Auctioneers' Offices: 31, Queen - street, Cardiff.
k751

ELY-CARDIFF AUCTION MARKET.
SALE THIS DAY at 10.30 a.m.
SETH PHILLIPS and SON.
k296

ELY-CARDIFF MARKET.
IMPORTANT SALE OF DAIRY COWS AND PEDIGREE LICENSED BULLS.
SATURDAY, 25th APRIL, 1936,
At Twelve Noon.

30 EXCELLENT DAIRY COWS,

comprising:—15 Choice Dairy Cows with Calves at foot and 15 Grand Springers; 4 Dairy Bulls, being 2 Pedigree Hereford Bulls (15 months old), 2 Pedigree Shorthorn Bulls (15 months old)—all licensed for service.
These Cattle are from the Best Dairying Districts of Ireland, and can be thoroughly recommended.
TERMS—CASH.
SETH PHILLIPS and SON,
Auctioneers. Offices: 18, Quay-street, Cardiff (Tel. 755), and at Pontllanfraith.
k298

70, QUEEN-STREET, CARDIFF.
SALE by AUCTION of the COSTLY and WELL-PRESERVED HOUSEHOLD FURNI-
TURE, CARPETS, SILVER, OIL-PAINT-

Ely cattle market advertisement, 21 April 1936. Situated in Norbury Road, Ely (now regarded as part of Fairwater) the market was established here because of its proximity to Ely station. Lougher's bacon factory was next-door. Before a formal market was created, a major event for the buying and selling of cattle locally was the annual Ely fair held on Magdalene's Day (22 July) with a winter fair on 11 December.

Charles Thorne (left), brickworks-owner's son and Leo Osmond, quarry-owner's son, pictured outside Windsor House, Cowbridge Road in 1910.

Daisy and Jess Denning (left) and Mr and Mrs Adams, outside Riverside Terrace in the early 1900s.

Highmead House, 1921. Highmead House was built in the late 1850s by William Vachell who was a Cardiff councillor. In 1860, he was killed in a coaching accident and by the following year Frederick Vachell, his wife and one daughter had taken up residence. They had seven servants: a housekeeper, cook, nurse, page, groom, gardener and housemaid. The grounds of the house were quite extensive and included vegetable gardens, lawns, an orchard and an ornamental pond. The house stayed in the ownership of the Vachells until the First World War when it was purchased by Edgar Edwards, a ship-owner [see page 119]. He lost much of his money in the depression of the 1920s and sold the house to the Hutchinson family. By 1930 it had been sold again, to a group of people setting up the Ely Garden City Club, which later became the West End Social Club. The West End moved to Ash Villa having sold Highmead House and its grounds on 4 May 1936 for £13,000. Soon after this, the house was demolished to make way for council houses in Highmead and Aberthaw roads and Fonmon Crescent.

Edgar Edwards, his family, staff and their families photographed at the back of Highmead House in 1920.

Left: Mr Springham and his dog Monty at the back entrance of Highmead House (on the main road) where the fruit and vegetable gardens were situated, 1921. Right: the head gardener, Mr A. Springham, 1921. The outdoor staff included four gardeners and a chauffeur at this time.

Miss Springham in the garden of Highmead House, 1921. She was allowed to stay at the house to keep the owner's niece company.

Mr and Mrs Springham and their daughter outside Bowen's Row, 1920. Bowen's Row stood on the site occupied today by the Silver Jubilee cottages on the corner of Cowbridge Road West and Grand Avenue. The row was also known as Britway or Brickway Terrace. The terrace was built in the 1850s, with William Bowen, his wife, three children, a servant and two apprentice carpenters recorded as residents of one of the eight houses in 1861. Other occupations of people living in the terrace at this time included: wheelwright, schoolmaster, brewer, foreman on iron wharf, labourer, blacksmith, and gateman. The terrace was included in the Highmead House Estate which was sold to Cardiff Corporation in 1936.

Cottage at Caerau, 21 October 1888. The artist and nineteenth-century Glamorgan historian, David Jones of Wallington, had been sketching in the locality using William Thomas's diary as a guide.

Cottage at the lower end of Church Road, Caerau, 1920. This cottage is possibly that shown in the sketch by David Jones on the previous page (end gable on right).

The same cottage forty years later in 1960 before the Heol Trelai carriageway was built.

Church Farm, as the name suggests, was situated close to St Mary's church at the top of the hill. It was home to the Thurston brothers, from left to right: Sid, Bert, William, George and Fred. The house became unoccupied in the 1930s and fell into ruin.

Gamekeeper's Lodge, 'the Round House', Cwrt-yr-Ala Park. On the south side of St Mary's Hill, Cwrt-yr-Ala Road led to Penylan Farm and an entrance to the Cwrt-yr-Ala estate in Michaelston-le-Pit. Local legend has it that one of the gamekeepers who lived at this lodge was found dead with no obvious signs of injury except for the marks of a cat on his back; he had earlier shot a cat belonging to an old woman from Cadoxton who was rumoured to be a witch! The lodge was then rebuilt as a circular house, the story goes, so the devil could not find a corner to hide in.

The Dusty Forge, which as this 1875 photograph shows, could still tend to your horse while you took refreshment next-door. There appears to be no record when The Dusty Forge was built, although in 1762, William Thomas refers to a Thomas Richard, 'late of Dusty Forge, Innkeeper'. There is no evidence that mail coaches used it as a regular stop, as after leaving The Angel Hotel in Cardiff the next stop was The Bear Inn at Cowbridge. It is possible that extra horses were put on to help up the steep hill at the Tumble. In 1791, William Thomas records the death of the 48-year-old John Williams, the Dusty Forge innkeeper who died 'from little pain... but weakness, and his body, especially his vitals weared out by his overmuch drinking'.

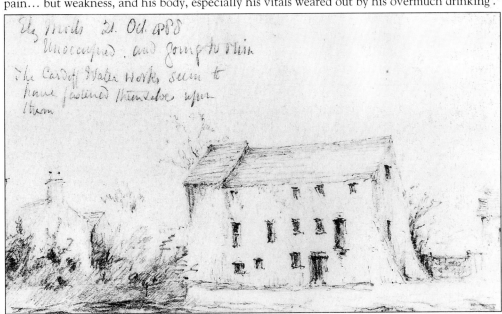

Ely Mills, 21 October 1888. Another David Jones sketch to which he has added, 'Unoccupied and going to ruin. The Cardiff Water Works seem to have fastened themselves upon them'. Little remains to be seen of the mills today, only the course of the mill race – from the weir on the River Ely to Birdies Lane (Cartwright Lane) off Plymouth Wood Road, the corn mill being situated at this point. A corn mill had stood on this site since the twelfth century.

A record onion crop at Palmer's market garden in 1919, looking in the direction of Ely Racecourse and Leckwith Woods. This business was started by Mr J. Palmer at the turn of the century and remained in operation until 1967 when the remaining land was sold for building. Earlier, parts of the market garden had been sold off for private housing developments. These included Arles Road, where although the first houses were erected before 1939 the last were not completed until 1953, work having been suspended during the war and its immediate aftermath.

Palmer's greenhouses. The driveway to the market garden is virtually the route of Barnard Avenue today, to the rear of St David's church.

Highfields Public House 1984. The pub was formerly Caerau farmhouse and the now demolished Jacrow Square adjacent was the extent of the farms garden and orchard. In 1881 Mr Edward Thomas is recorded as living at Caerau Farm with his wife, three children and also three general servants, three farm servants and a gardener. Some five years later Mr Thomas was leaving his 300-acre farm, and a local paper advertising the sale stated 'the whole of his cattle, sheep, horses and implements [consisted] of 53 cattle including several useful milking cows and heifers, in and with calf, 11 two year old steers, 20 yearling cattle and 11 calves, 50 useful Radnor ewes and lambs, 18 cart and other horses, sow and 6 pigs, 3 storers and a boar. Also a large and useful assortment of implements, poultry, portions of household furniture and the dairy utensils'.

Glynteg Hall, Station Terrace, 1984. One of the oldest houses in the Ely area, it now provides office headquarters for the Royal College of Nursing. In the 1820s it was home for the Thomases. The members of this family, notably Mrs Elizabeth Thomas, were prominent workers for Methodism in Ely. Her husband, John Thomas, was a maltster and some brewing was carried out at Glynteg Hall making it the first brewery in Ely. John Thomas died in 1842 and Elizabeth Thomas later moved to the Castle Brewery in Great Frederick Street, Cardiff. The house subsequently became offices for the Ely Brewery.

View from St Mary's Hill. Fields are all that can be seen beyond the Caerau brickworks in this photograph [see pages 58 and 77 for later views]. Looking towards Cardiff most of the fields were part of Ely Farm, run by George Thomas in the last century.

Left: George Thomas, c. 1890. He took over Ely Farm from his father in 1843 and was to hold the office of Constable of Kibbor, the official of the 'Hundred' to whom the parish constables were responsible. The 'Hundred' was an ancient administrative sub-division of the county. In his diary in the 1890s, Thomas noted that his workmen received £1 1s per week, a calf was sold for £1 0s and the rent on the farm for half a year was £50. In 1895, George died and his son Illtyd took over Ely Farm. Illtyd was a civil engineer, chartered surveyor and auctioneer. He was made a councillor in 1885, alderman in 1905, Lord Mayor 1907-1908 and knighted in 1925. In 1930, Sir Illtyd Thomas left the farm, which was taken over by the Davies family who concentrated on dairy products. Right: George Thomas's wife, c. 1890.

Three

Industrialisation
and Ely

Ely remained virtually unchanged for hundreds of years with the inhabitants depending on the land for their livelihood. In 1841, when the population of Ely was 224, most of the villagers were agricultural labourers in addition to one weaver, blacksmith, horse-breaker, tiler, shoemaker, carpenter, victualler, wheelwright and hay-merchant. By the middle of the last century the main settlement was around Ely Bridge with Station Terrace, Windsor Terrace (in Cowbridge Road opposite The White Lion), and Grover's Terrace (Nos 70-100, Mill Road) forming the westward extension of the Ely hamlet. Ely was separated from Canton at this time by Ely Common.

If there was one event that can be said to have impacted on Ely more than any other it was the coming of the railway in 1850, which linked South and West Wales with Bristol and London. The first train ran through Ely on 18 June (Waterloo Day) and 17 days later on 5 July 1850 the Cardiff and Merthyr Guardian announced the end of the stage coaches: 'The Bristol and Swansea mailcoaches ceases to run from this day. The letterbags will hence forth be conveyed by the South Wales Railway'. A journey by stage coach from Newport to Cowbridge took 3¾ hours.

Ely station opened in early September 1850 and a letter to the Cardiff and Merthyr Guardian on 6 February 1858 gave a picture of its importance as 'not only a focal despatch point for livestock but also a passenger station of no mean importance used by the inhabitants of Llandaff, Whitchurch, Fairwater, Radyr, Ely and all those villages and country houses bordering on the turnpike road for six miles westwards' [see page 120].

Forty years after the 1841 census Ely's population had doubled to 454 with 160 people originating from outside Glamorgan, and showed a new variety of occupations such as railway labourers, porters, engine drivers, coal merchants, paper mill and brewery workers. Although there was a growth in market gardens the drift of workers away from the land and into the factories continued with the arrival of a second brewery, Crosswells, and Chivers pickle factory in 1900.

Further developments were taking place in order to cope with the expanding population – The White Lion was demolished and rebuilt in 1892, St David's church opened in 1871 and the church hall in 1897, some distance away in Clarke Street. Opposite the hall, Ely's first council school (Millbank) opened in 1902. Civic amenities were provided with about 20 acres of Ely Common being opened to the public as Victoria Park in 1897.

In the Parishes of Caerau and Michaelston-super-Ely little had changed at the turn of the century. However, the building of the Barry Railway on the edge of the parishes brought a population increase to Saintwell, with cottages spread along the main road. In 1890, in response to this growth, Mr William Windsor built a large shed of wood and iron as a 'navvies mission' on the corner of the lane leading to Cwrt-yr-Ala. Everything was to change after the First World War and most of all the rural character of the area with the growing demands for housing to provide 'Homes fit for Heroes'.

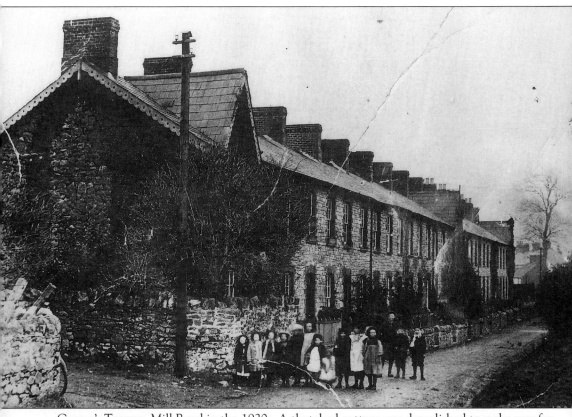

Grover's Terrace, Mill Road in the 1920s. A thatched cottage was demolished to make way for the terraced houses built by I.B.K. Grover to cater for the growing workforce being attracted by the new industries.

The railway had brought new jobs, new people and the English language to the area. The Wesleyan chapel in Mill Road began to hold services in Welsh and English from 1858. Other changes began to take place around Ely village. The Ely Pumping Station was opened by the Cardiff Water Works Company in 1852. Although brewing had been carried out on a small scale at Glynteg Hall, the first major brewery began in 1853 which developed into Tower Brewery. Ely Racecourse opened its gates on 30 May 1855, Cardiff Union Industrial School (Ely Hospital) was built in 1862 and Ely Paper Mill was in production in 1865. While these developments were substantial, according to the 1878 Wales Register and Guide of each town parish and village in North and South Wales, Ely was still 'a small village in the parish of Llandaff about two miles from Cardiff, having a railway station, extensive paper works and a brewery'.

At the time this photograph was taken, houses had been built in Clarke Street on the opposite side of Cowbridge Road. It was as early as 3 October 1917 that the Llandaff and Dinas Powis Rural District Council were looking for sites where housing for 'the working classes' could be built. By 29 April 1919, the area abutting Clarke Street had been identified and soon after it was agreed to build 12 houses per acre on it. The chief valuer and the Plymouth Estate who owned the site finally agreed a total price of £950 and the council borrowed £13,500 to build fifteen houses. People were in the houses by February 1922 when the council gave permission 'to erect a motor cycle shed at No. 22 Clarke Street' and a fowl-house at No. 20 'providing that the birds were confined to the pen and not allowed to stray and annoy the neighbours'.

Mr and Mrs William Davies and family at the rear of houses in Cowbridge Road, 1900. Mr Davies, senior (with the beard) is standing behind his wife, seated centre. Mr and Mrs Emanuel Davies, grocers of Riverside Terrace, are on the right of the picture.

Mr Percy (left) and John Lloyd in Mill Road, 1920s. The cyclist and his friend were both regulars at The White Lion. Mr Lloyd also used to play drums in the Salvation Army band.

Old cottages in Mill Road. These were demolished in the 1930s to make way for St Clare's Roman Catholic church which in turn has been replaced by a doctor's surgery and chemist.

Cottage and shoe shop (next to the old Wesleyan chapel) in Mill Road. At the chapel's opening in 1858 [see page 85] many gifts were received, including a silver communion jug, cup and plate, each bearing the inscription: 'Presented to the Welsh Wesleyan Chapel, Ely, by Mrs. Thomas of Glyn Teg Hall A.D. 1857'.

Mill Road and Cowbridge Road junction, 1906. On one corner stands The White Lion with E. Davies' grocer and butcher on the other side. Reminiscing back to the 1880s Ivor Harris recalls the remnants of a diamond-shaped village green bordered on the west side by a cobbled pavement. Overlooking the green was a row of four to five thatched cottages with front gardens that could only be entered by getting over a stone stile.

Mill Road, 1928. This house, which can be seen in the previous photograph, stood between a drapery shop run by Jessie James and a fish and chip shop owned by Mr and Mrs Dale and their daughter Queenie.

Rear garden, Riverside Terrace, early 1930s. Playing out the back are Joan Smith (top), Mavis Gregory (née Codd) and Lawton Smith.

Windsor Terrace, Cowbridge Road, 1913. This terrace, named after the ground landlord, Baroness Windsor of the Plymouth family, can be seen today minus its front gardens, opposite The White Lion public house.

Isabel and Gladys Niblett in Station Terrace, 1907. This street was built in the 1850s to cope with the influx of workers on the railway and in the other new industries. This can be illustrated by the record of occupations undertaken by residents in 1880: one police constable, one railway signalman, three labourers at the paper mills, one railway plate-layer and one agricultural labourer.

Mill Road in flood, 1927. This part of Ely flooded regularly until the river was straightened out in the 1940s. The height of the floodwater on this occasion was recorded as 39 inches on the post office wall. The Ely branch of the Candle King store can be seen on the left. Candle King had stores throughout Cardiff: in James Street, Carlisle Street, Crwys Road, North Road, Albany Road and Clifton Street.

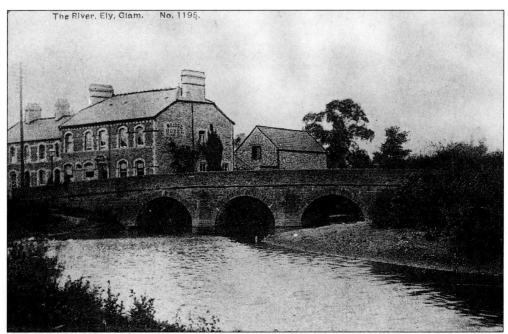

The old river bridge and The Bridge Inn, *c.* 1900. The bridge had been rebuilt in 1832 with four arches.

The new bridge, *c.* 1911. This was built at a cost of £4,896. The Caerau-with-Ely parish magazine for July 1911 stated: 'The Lord Mayor of Cardiff, Mr Jenkins opened the bridge on Friday June 16th 1911 and presented Mr Edward Sydenham with a certificate from the Royal Humane Society as a reward for having on the 23rd March 1911 gone to the rescue of a child who was in imminent danger of drowning and whose life he gallantly saved'. The newsletter continued: 'There were very few Ely people present at the function and it seemed almost as if it did not concern them but nearly the whole of the juvenile population were there so much as to call forth a remark on the subject from the Lord Mayor'.

The old bridge, *c*. 1910. The Bridge Hotel can be seen in its 1877 rebuilt form. The 1851 census lists Mary Lewis as licensee of the Ely Bridge Inn. As well as keeping the public house she also farmed 8 acres.

The new bridge, *c*. 1915. The same view some five years later; the main difference, apart from the new bridge, is the realignment of the main road along its present course.

The White Lion Inn in 1892, two years before its rebuilding by Edwin Edmunds of Llandaff. The White Lion has now closed as a public house and is being converted into flats. In 1851, the pub was being run by Edward and Mary Laut, their son and two housemaids. Mr Laut was described as a publican and farmer owning three acres and employing two men.

The new White Lion, c. 1900. Built with a view to accommodating racegoers at the nearby course, part of the main road frontage also included Trelai House. 'Trelai' was a Victorian attempt to give the area a Welsh place name (the correct form is 'Elai').

The Red Lion, 1984. Three lions could be found in the Llandaff parish: The White Lion and Red Lion in Ely and The Black Lion in Llandaff village. Towards the end of its life The Red Lion had the appearance of a workers' pub (for the nearby Whitbread Brewery). With the closure of the brewery the pub was sold and is now a freehouse called The Coach House.

Mrs Winter, tenant of The Red Lion pub, Station Terrace 1915. Her husband was the head brewer at Ely Brewery. Mrs Winter supplied clay pipes on the pub counter for the use of customers who would dip them in their beer before use.

A watercolour of Ely Brewery by F. Viner, 1900. [See text on page 67 relating to brewing at Ely].

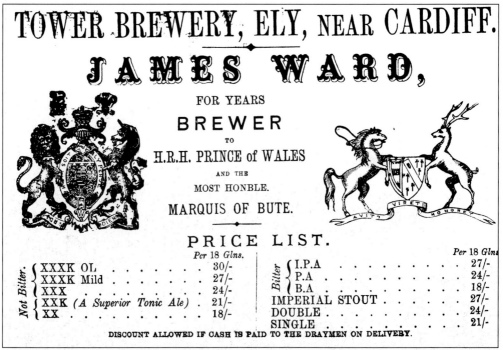

TOWER BREWERY, ELY, NEAR CARDIFF.

JAMES WARD,

FOR YEARS

BREWER

TO

H.R.H. PRINCE of WALES

AND THE

MOST HONBLE.

MARQUIS OF BUTE.

PRICE LIST.

		Per 18 Glns.			Per 18 Glns.
Not Bitter. {	XXXX OL	30/-	**Bitter** { I.P.A		27/-
	XXXX Mild	27/-	P.A		24/-
	XXX	24/-	B.A		18/-
	XXX (*A Superior Tonic Ale*)	21/-	IMPERIAL STOUT		27/-
	XX	18/-	DOUBLE		24/-
			SINGLE		21/-

DISCOUNT ALLOWED IF CASH IS PAID TO THE DRAYMEN ON DELIVERY.

Tower Brewery was opened by James Ward, whose prices are shown in this advertisement from *Butchers Cardiff and Swansea Directory 1875-6*.

ELY PAPER WORKS

Ely Paper Works was founded by Brown and Evans in 1865 and originally covered an area of about eight acres. Rags were used to make 'half-stuff' which was sent to England. In 1875 Ely Paper Works went into liquidation, and was bought in 1877 by Thomas Owen who installed new machines and production increased to 80 tons a week during the next year. Twenty-two people were employed in 1877; a machine man's wage for a working week of 72 hours was 30s, and a sorter earned 12s to 15s for the same hours. By 1896 production had risen to 400 tons a week, and the mill was the largest producer of newsprint in Britain, able to support a newspaper circulation of ten million copies a week. It was one of the first mills in Britain to use woodpulp; the firm owned its own woodpulp mills in Sweden and Norway. In 1910 a swimming pool was added to the mill's amenities, but was infilled in 1982.

In 1933, the famous 'Ely Newsprint' was discontinued, and the production of esparto paper was greatly increased. In 1936, the Lord Mayor of Cardiff officially started the production of a parchmenting machine – at the time the largest machine of its kind in the world. In 1947, the Mill Road sports ground was bought and in 1956 Wiggins Teape acquired the licence to manufacture the revolutionary NCR paper. Their recently acquired mill at Ely proved to be the ideal factory to produce the paper. In recent years a number of demergers and mergers resulted in Wiggins Teape becoming Arjo Wiggins Appleton. The company is now the third largest paper manufacturer in Europe and the world's largest producer of carbonless paper. The Ely mill contributes significantly to the world's paper production.

Ely Paper Works, 1880. This is an early retouched photograph showing the original buildings started by Brown and Evans in 1865 and extended by Thomas Owen in 1877.

Ely Industrial School, early 1900s. Ely Hospital was built in 1862 on its present site as an industrial school and workhouse for orphans and poor children. It was built by Mr David Jones of Penarth at a cost of about £3,000, the land having been bought from Baroness Windsor for £700. In 1875 it was described as follows: 'The building affords accommodation for 320 children who are educated and taught – the boys simple trades, the girls to make their own clothes and to undertake any positions as servants. When they leave the school they are supplied with two new suits of clothes and other requisites but nothing that would in any way indicate they had been inmates in a workhouse'. The Industrial School was part of the Cardiff Union which controlled the workhouses, and was known as 'Ely Lodge.' St David's Hospital, which was an adult workhouse, was called 'Cardiff Lodge.'

Ely Lodge never became an adult workhouse and in 1905, the Ely Cottage Children's Home was added by the Cardiff Union. In 1930 the hospital became the responsibility of the Public Assistance Committee until 1948, when it was transferred to the National Health Service as a psychiatric hospital. The change in emphasis from industrial school to psychiatric hospital seems to have been gradual. The patients worked in the hospital allotment gardens in Arles Road and there was a piggery fronting the main road where the fire station is today. The patients made handstitched carpets, chainlink fencing and brushes.

Ely Cottage Children's Home, c. 1910.

Ely Hospital staff in the dining room, 1922. Matron Moore is in the plain clothes.

Ely Hospital staff with Dr and Mrs Payne in the centre (seated) and Mr Hall who was the master of the children's home (seated far left). Lady and Sir Charles Melhuish are seated next to Dr Payne.

Continued from previous page: In 1948 Ely Hospital changed its emphasis to providing care for people with learning difficulties. But in 1967 it found itself the subject of a parliamentary enquiry – the Howe Report – receiving national TV and press coverage. Although the report was hard for the people who had lived and worked there, there were some positive consequences such as an increase in resources being made available nationwide. In 1984 the All Wales strategy for people with learning disabilities was launched. Since then many hospital residents have moved to live in houses within local communities. It is planned that the number of residents will continue to diminish until 1999, the target date for closure.

Mr Ernest David by his shop on Cowbridge Road East on the corner of Aldsworth Road. The site was until recently a Comet warehouse but currently stands empty.

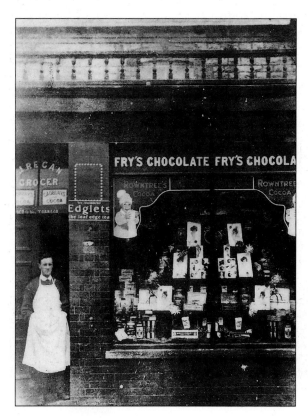

Regan's grocer's shop, No. 4 Riverside Terrace, *c.* 1910. Mr Regan stands at the doorway. Next door was Peach's drapery shop.

Caerau House, 1979. Completed around 1903, this house had been erected by Sir Edward S. Hill KSB, one time MP for Bristol South, and managing director of Hill's Dry Dock, Cardiff. At the time of his death in 1904, Hill's freehold estate in Ely and Caerau comprised some 255 acres of pasture and woodland, situated south of the Cowbridge Road and Caerau Lane. The property included a large farm used for horse-rearing and the house pictured above. In 1904 the house was occupied by his son, Vernon Hill, a well-known cricketer in his day who played for Somerset and was a member of the MCC. Built near the house was the isolation hospital, which in 1947 became a geriatric hospital and is today a hostel. Caerau House then became a residence for staff working at the hospital. If it were still standing today a good viewpoint would be had from the new Ely Link Road but it was demolished soon after this photograph was taken.

Class at Ely Council School in Clarke Street, pictured c. 1913. This was the first school to be opened in the Ely area (1902). It is now called Millbank Primary School.

Fairwater Road, Ely, c. 1910. Although now regarded as Fairwater, Fairwater Road (now St Fagans Road) was once considered part of Ely, as was the nearby cattle market and the brewery. It is difficult to determine the exact boundary of Ely on the 'internal' side as it is part of the Llandaff parish. The official acreage of Ely was 474.

Ely Pumping Station, 1984. A direct consequence of the 1849 cholera outbreak in the town of Cardiff was the sinking of wells at Ely and the construction of a pumping station by the Cardiff Water Works Company. The building in the photograph is actually the later (1877) coal store which had living accommodation above for the station superintendent and his family.

Pumping engine in the Welsh Industrial & Maritime Museum, Cardiff. This is the original engine that was delivered to Ely in 1851, pumping the water from the wells and then through pipes to a storage reservoir at Penhill. The water was then fed by gravity to the centre of Cardiff. Designed by James Simpson and built at Hayle, Cornwall, it started pumping on 12 January 1852 and continued until the 1920s when Ely became a reserve supply. Today, the modern pumping station provides a contract supply to Aberthaw power station.

Henry Jenkins. The Cardiff Water Works Company acquired the water rights to the Corn Mill in 1850. It was only the water supply they were interested in and, the mill itself soon became abandoned, hence David Jones' comment, 'unoccupied and going to ruin' in 1888. One of the last millers was John Jenkins, whose son, Henry Michael Jenkins, was born nearby at Fairwater Cottage. After his father's death the family moved to Swansea and by 1854 Henry was working in Bristol. Through studying in his own time, he became secretary and editor for the Royal Agricultural Society in 1868. He died on Christmas Eve, 1886.

SOUTH WALES RAILWAY.

O N and after MONDAY, the 2nd SEPTEMBER, the Stations at

| MARSHFIELD, | PENCOED, and |
| ELY, | BRITTON FERRY, |

will be Opened for Passengers and Parcels.

The Intermediate Stoppages between Chepstow and Swansea will, therefore, in some cases be altered.

Train Bills will be ready for delivery at all Stations on the 30th inst.

A Goods Train will also run daily (Sundays excepted) between Chepstow and Swansea, in both directions, calling at Newport, Cardiff, Llantrissant, Bridgend, Port Talbot, and Neath.

Rates of Carriage and all particulars can be learnt on application at the Stations.

FREDERICK CLARKE, Superintendent.

Chepstow Terminus, 27th August, 1850.

The opening of Ely station. The South Wales Railway was opened from Swansea to Chepstow on 18 June 1850. Engineered by Isambard Kingdom Brunel, this broad gauge (7 ft 0$\frac{1}{4}$in) railway was to form part of the trunk route from London to Fishguard. Although Ely station opened on 2 September 1850 though communication eastward to London had to wait until the completion of the Wye bridge at Chepstow in July 1852 [see page 120].

Ely station staff, 1910-11. Ely was an important station, with considerable goods traffic from sidings into Ely Paper Mill and the breweries, and was particularly busy on race days with spectators and racehorses arriving by rail. In the 1939 (10 and 11 April) race programme five trains were listed between 12.24 and 1.30 for those wishing to enjoy the day's racing.

Four

Creating
a new community

The Cardiff Housing and Town Planning Committee was set up immediately after the First World War. The council minutes in November 1918 state that the issue of housing was one of 'extreme urgency' after the local government board requested 400 extra houses should be built. The land belonging to Green Farm and Red House Farm became a target as it seemed ideal land for building. A compulsory purchase order was made on 26 January 1920, and a price of £40,000 was agreed for Red House Farm and land, and a further £32,000 for Green Farm. There was extreme urgency to begin building and, two years before Ely was taken inside the Cardiff City boundary, the housing committee instructed the City Engineer in July 1920 'to forthwith open up the quarry on this land [Red House] with a view to providing a supply of stones for the new roads'.

House building began in earnest in 1921 and 1922 with Caerau Square being some of the first houses to be built, along with streets around Red House Farm such as Archer Road, Frank Road, Llewelyn Avenue, Pethybridge Road, Ty Coch Road and the lower end of Grand Avenue. The site was referred to as Ely Garden Suburbs, reflecting the Hertfordshire garden cities built some years before. 'In the gabled cottages, the low housing densities and the baroque patterns of the road layouts Ely is a good example of this ideal'. By 1924 some 3,412 new houses had been built.

Cardiff Corporation was experimenting at this time with various building materials: wooden, concrete, brick and metal houses were all built. However, as one resident of the concrete houses around Caerau Square remembers: '[in] the houses, though nice and roomy, the great fault was concrete; even the bedroom floors were concrete, too cold in winter and too hot in summer'.

By the 1930s houses had been erected as far west as Green Farm Road with infilling in such areas as Pendine and Highmead Road. The first batch of major building south of Cowbridge Road West occurred in 1936 with the Amroth Road area being constructed. With so many new houses, new schools, churches and shops were to follow: Herbert Thompson School was opened on 2 May 1927, Windsor Clive on 6 September 1929, St Francis' Roman Catholic School (beginning in the church hall doubling as a church) on 3 October 1927, and Hywel Dda on St David's Day, 1934. The four main churches were also built comparatively quickly: Ely United Reformed Church (foundation stone laid on 7 September 1926), Ely Gospel Hall (9 October 1930), Church of the Resurrection (9 October 1934), and Archer Road Baptist Church (13 September 1928) [see page 86]. This indicates the pace at which the population was expanding.

Having built on much of the land north of Cowbridge Road West, the City Council turned its attention to the comparatively rural area of Saintwell and Caerau. In February 1939 Sweldon Farm was bought at auction for £12,400 although the sale did not include the farmhouse and 18 acres. After the Second World War a few 'prefabs' were built, but soon modern developments took place with the creation of Heol Trelai which linked Saintwell, Caerau and the Amroth Road area. Much of the ground surrounding Ely Racecourse was built upon, and by the 1960s, apart from a few small infillings, Ely was complete. Since that time modern private estates have been built on the fringes of Ely at St Fagans Court, the Culverhouse Farm area, Cwrt-yr-Ala Lane, Saintwell and later more council houses on Sweldon Hill. Of course, building never ends, and in the last ten years houses have been built along the Drope Road and in the green fields of Michaelston-super-Ely.

Aerial view, 1948. In this photograph the northern part of Ely is virtually complete as far as street lay-outs are concerned. South of the Cowbridge Road, which runs diagonally across the photograph, Heol Trelai has yet to be built and RAF Llandaff with its barrage-balloon hangars can be clearly seen in the centre of the picture.

Group of workmen, pictured outside 17 Aberthaw Road during the building of the north Ely housing estate in 1935-6. Fifteen years earlier in 1921 Cardiff City Housing Department had issued a schedule of basic prices for the Ely Housing Scheme. Labourers such as bricklayers, masons, slaters, tilers, carpenters and joiners were to be paid 2s 4d per hour, while a plumber received an extra $\frac{1}{2}$d per hour. The most expensive was the use of a horse, cart and man at 4s per hour. The materials included cement at 15s per bag, tar at 10d a gallon, dressers complete with fasteners at £8 6s 6d and lavatory basins with $\frac{1}{2}$ inch hot and cold taps, plus waste chain, overflow bracket and frame supports at £2 15s.

The Ely Housing Department of Cardiff City Council on their annual outing in the 1920s.

Left: Mrs King on a motor-cycle in Caerau Square, 1929. Right: Marjorie, Colin and Billy King also in Caerau Square, c. 1926. Despite its name, Caerau Square was actually in Ely and was built largely on what had been Red House Farm's twelve-acre field.

Caerau Square, August 1961. Situated where St David's Crescent and Cymric Close now stand, work on Caerau Square was begun just after the end of the First World War by private contractors, but was to be completed by the council. The American Roller Rink which originally stood in Westgate Street was dismantled and re-erected in Mill Road, where it was used as a concrete-casting depot to build the Caerau Square houses. It was first known as 'No. 9 Road' and in 1922 the first residents moved in. Surrounded by fields the square was linked to the main road by a footpath that was formed by the comings and goings of residents. Later the council built a road leading to the square.

Caerau Square, 18 April 1963. In the 1920s and '30s, the lighting was provided by gas lamps, which stood in brackets on the walls and were run off a mains supply, paid for by means of a meter which took pennies and shillings. Even the square itself was lit by gas lamps, the gasman coming round each evening to light them. The average weekly rent for such a house was 12s. When Caerau Square was first built the shopping facilities were poor. A single bus used to take people to Canton and back each week and this was where all the main shopping was done. The residents of the square sometimes opened small shops in their houses to meet the local demand: Mr Patreane opened the first shop, and this was later followed by shops run by the Murrell family and the Bruno family. The condition of the houses in Caerau Square deteriorated rapidly after the war. Many people complained of leaks and dampness and the square was condemned as unfit and demolished in 1963.

Redevelopment of the Caerau Square site, 11 October 1963, where 148 new houses with new addresses were built.

Grand Avenue, showing the drinking fountain. Laid out in the garden city tradition, 'The Grand Avenue' (as it was actually named) had been designed to accommodate a planned extension of the tramway from Victoria Park in the central reservation. By 1929, however the plan had been abandoned. Trolley-buses, of course did run in Ely and the poles they used can be clearly seen in the photograph.

Mr M. Patreane and nephew Keith. The Patreanes ran the first shop on the new estate – first from a temporary shop in Caerau Square and then in Grand Avenue (next to the URC church).

Cwrt-yr-Ala Road in the early 1960s. Cwrt-yr-Ala Road extended up to the city boundary before turning into Heol-yr-Odyn. Behind this section of Heol-yr-Odyn can be seen the piggery run by the Millward family.

Haig Place during its construction, 1938-9. Earl Haig houses were reserved for servicemen and their families. Haig Place is situated off Green Farm Road near its junction with Cowbridge Road West.

Caerau brickworks, 14 October 1949. This view from St Mary's Hill shows the construction of houses on Heol Carnau [see also page 77]. The Ely Link Road now runs below the escarpment on the right.

Prefab bungalow in Heol-yr-Odyn, c. 1940. These homes were to be replaced by a new kind of 'Swedish-type' prefabricated house in the early 1970s. In the aerial photo on page 52 the lay-out of the pre-fabs can be seen around this and the Caerau Lane area.

Wilson Road shops, early 1930s. Stork's, seen on the corner, was one of the oldest family concerns in Ely.

The opening of the Star Supply Stores, Wilson Road, 1925.

Inside the 'Little White Shop', No. 2 Cowbridge Road showing Mrs Ellis on the left and Miss Wilson on the right. The shop was owned and run by Miss Wilson from 1923 to 1966. It had previously been a butcher's.

H.C. Lane the baker, Clarke Street, 1929. The first baker's shop in Ely, it had a separate bakehouse to the rear where locals would bring their Christmas cakes to be baked for 1 shilling.

Crowley's grocery shop, Caerau Road, 1959. The shop was acquired by the Highfields public house next-door and incorporated into a skittle alley.

The Dusty Forge Inn, *c.* 1925. In 1841 Catherine Benjamin was the publican here; she was a widow with six children, the eldest of whom was a blacksmith's apprentice. Also living in the inn was a female servant and a lodger who was a blacksmith. Listed separately in the census returns was the forge itself, where John Jenkins, a carpenter lived with his three children. By 1925, the Dusty was advertising itself as serving 'teas' and the blacksmith's had expanded to serve the motor trade. It remained a pub until the early 1990s when it was closed. In 1996 it is being refurbished to become an Ely young people's resource centre.

Ely Flower Show committee, 1920s. The show was held each August in a field near the old part of St Fagans Road.

Ely Garden City Club (West End), c. 1930. The photograph shows the founder members who purchased Highmead House in 1930. The club later became the West End Social Club moving a short distance west along the Cowbridge Road to Ash Villa where it continues today.

D. Emery and R. Heereman of Ely Council School (Millbank), Welsh schoolboy internationals, 1933-34.

Trelai Junior School football team, winners of the Stanbury Cup, 1951-52.

Standards 6-7 and ex-7 at Ely Council School (Millbank), 1925-26. Among those pictured, from left to right, back row: ? Hall, ? Mundell, ? Norman, Alf Gardner, Fred Taysome, Dick Crook, Harold Hodges, Roy Callow. Third row: Bill Durham, ? Griffin, ? Ginn, ? Rees, ? Thomas, ? Barnett, Dick Jones, Edgar Harling. Arthur Lippiat. Front row: G. Mason, ? Cross, Arthur ?, V. Shore, R.W. Budd, G. Davies, Walter Rowe, ? Venables, ? Vowles, Sid Godbeer, ? Garret.

Windsor Clive School, 1932.

Trelai Junior School class photograph, 1959.

Coronation celebrations at Windsor Clive Infants' School, June 1953.

Pethybridge Hall was built by unemployed volunteers in the 1930s. The photograph shows one of two foundation stones being laid. It reads: 'laid by A.E. Bush representing the voluntary workers of the scheme. Feb 15th. 1933'. A similar stone on the other side of the original main entrance was laid by Cardiff's Lord Mayor, Alderman C.F. Sanders JP on behalf of the donors. The hall was a community facility for use by Ely residents but by the mid-1970s it was underused and in need of modernisation. Once again, the unemployed, this time on a job creation programme, undertook the work. The hall is now a youth as well as a community facility and is run by the Community Education Department of Cardiff County Council. Over the years the centre has built up strong ties with Stammheim youth centre in Stuttgart and a mural outside the main entrance portrays these links.

Army hut squatters, Ely Racecourse. Immediately after the end of the Second World War an acute shortage of houses forced some people to squat in the old army huts that had been abandoned after the war.

Five

Working in the Western Suburbs

BREWING AT ELY

The first purpose-built brewery in Ely dates from around 1855 when David Davies leased from Lord Romilly a piece of land on which he built the Ely Brewery. By the mid-1860s Matthew Cross was brewing in Ely at 'Brewers House' and his trade card depicted a substantial number of buildings making up the brewery. In 1875 James Ward was calling the concern Tower Brewery but in 1887 the business was taken over by the Ely Brewery Co. Ltd. Meanwhile, in 1892, Crosswells Ltd was established using a large store in Penarth Road to promote and sell beers manufactured by Walter Showell and Sons Ltd of the Crosswells Brewery at Oldbury, Worcestershire. In 1897 a new brewery was built on the north side of the Cardiff to Swansea railway line and almost opposite the original Ely Brewery.

The Ely Brewery began to purchase pubs in Cardiff and then built on its initial success by buying more premises in the Valleys. In 1920 the Ely Brewery merged with Rhondda Valley Breweries Co. Ltd to form the Rhondda Valley and Ely Breweries Ltd and from 1928 to simply the Ely Brewery Co. Ltd. This merger made the company a dominant force within the valleys – 80 per cent of the brewery' pubs were in this area with the custom of hard-drinking miners being heavily relied upon. In 1926, however, the General Strike and the long Miners' Strike which followed had a major adverse effect on the company which a year later was unable to issue a dividend. Drastic action was required and within two years the Treherbert and Ponypridd breweries were closed and all production concentrated at Ely. The depression of the 1930s made matters worse and it was not until after the appointment in 1947 of Lazarus Nidditch as chairman that Ely Brewery declared a small dividend – the first for 21 years. Nidditch established a welfare hall and canteen within the brewery and outings were arranged for employees. He also set about improving the 250 pubs with new saloon bars and ladies' toilets! He introduced a range of new beers – Brewers Own, Golden Gleam and TV Ale which was aimed at the threat of television with the slogan 'when you're watching Wenvoe [the nearby broadcasting mast] you can still get Ely service'.

Meanwhile, Crosswells Brewery had become a subsidiary of Andrew Buchans Brewery Ltd of Rhymney in 1937 and in 1958 changed their name to Rhymney Breweries Ltd. On 16 December 1959 a merger with the Ely Brewery Co. was completed resulting in the creation of an 'empire' owning 730 pubs. It soon became apparent that it was uneconomic to run two separate breweries – Crosswells and Ely – on virtually one site and in 1963 the original Ely brewery was demolished ending over eighty years of brewing. In the meantime, a new extension, administrative offices and a canteen were built on the site of the old Ely cattle market.

In March 1966 Whitbreads made a successful bid for the company. However, in October 1977 the managing director of Whitbread Wales informed the Rhymney Brewery workforce that the brewery was to close the next year. The public's move away from ale to lager was one reason for the decision. The Ely Brewery continued brewing beer until April 1982 when it was closed and demolished to make way for housing; the brewery offices were taken over by South Wales Police in June 1989.

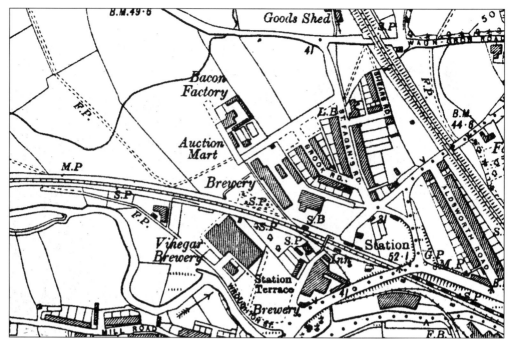

Map of old Ely, 1921, which shows Lougher's bacon factory and Ely Market (detailed as an auction mart) in the north. The two breweries are clearly visible as well as Chivers (vinegar brewery) with part of the paper mill showing in the bottom right-hand corner.

Brewery workers and lorries, 1950s.

Coopers at Ely Brewery, *c.* 1900. An old retired brewery worker, Mr Strong, stated that in 1912 he began work at the brewery as a stable boy. This job involved feeding the horses, mucking out and polishing the brasses – before breakfast! Then he would accompany the driver on a delivery and hold the horse's head outside the pub while the driver was inside having his lunch. The 14-year-old Mr Strong would be given some stone ginger ale to drink.

Brewery workers and lorries 1950's.

Brewery workers around 1950.

Left: a Crosswells beer-bottle label. Right: inset taken from the Ely Brewery Co. Ltd's price list when draught dark XXX was 1s 2d per pint and Brewers Own was 1s 4d per half-bottle not including a deposit on the bottle.

THE
PRIZE

RHONDDA VALLEY & ELY BREWERIES LTP

Left: a mid-1920s poster. Right: the original Ely Brewery in 1963, just before its demolition. The site is now occupied by a bottled gas depot.

The Whitbread brewery bottling plant being built in the 1960s.

The bottling plant within a year of its closure in 1981.

Aerial view of Ely Paper Mills, June 1930. The photograph shows Birchfield Crescent marked out but no houses yet built.

This machine had operated at Ely Paper Mills for almost a hundred years when it became obsolete in 1965.

Ely Paper Mills employees, 20 June 1908.

A general view of old salle No. 5 showing women sorting the paper by hand. This work involved going through the paper with a rubber thimble and taking out any cut or dirty pieces.

Ely Paper Mills experiencing the regular flooding of the River Ely, 1911. In 1948, following yet another flood, the paper mill claimed £85,000 damages from Cardiff Corporation which accepted responsibility, but contested the amount of damages.

A Great Western Railway (GWR) 2-6-0 Mogul class 4300, 3 November 1927. This Swansea to Cardiff stopping train is seen passing the paper mill during another flood of the River Ely.

Brickworks' employees, *c.* 1910. There were two brickworks in Ely; one was at the top of Church Road in Caerau which was owned by the Thorne family and the other in Heol Trelai (Highland Park) where the small industrial units now stand. The sites were chosen because the red marl in the cliffs was ideal for brick-making. By 1963 the Caerau works had closed but Highland Park was still employing 60 people (43 from Ely). The works had at one time specialised in highly glazed bricks but moved over to the 'common' brick which was in greater demand. During this time the cliff-face was blasted five times a day and 300,000 bricks were made per week. Highland Park brickworks finally closed around 1970.

Left: Thorne & Sons' brickworks, *c.* 1910, soon after traction engines replaced horses for transporting the bricks. Right: a brick manufactured by Thornes.

Caerau brickworks, 1948. Note the road lay-out beginning on the racecourse [see also page 58]. The first time the brickworks appears on the Ordnance Survey map (1921) it is called West End brickworks. The chimney of the Highland brickworks can be seen in the distance to the right.

A view of the Highland brickworks taken in June 1965. Heol Trelai is in the background running parallel to the brickworks. This is now the site of the Argyle Way industrial estate.

ALFRED LOUGHER & SON Ltd.

BACON AND HAM CURERS

SAUSAGE MANUFACTURERS, LARD
REFINERS, and SPECIALISTS IN ALL
CLASSES OF COOKED MEATS

NORBURY ROAD - ELY - CARDIFF

Telephone: LLANDAFF 150

Alfred Lougher & Sons advertisement. The original factory was built for Alfred Lougher & Sons around the turn of the century on a site bordering Llandaff, hence the original name – Llandaff Jam and Pickle Manufacturing Company. The original building was destroyed by fire in 1910 and a replacement erected on a site in Ely. At that time the company cured bacon and ham, baked pies and manufactured its famous sausages, from a still secret recipe. The products were sold through retail outlets, Cardiff indoor market and a factory shop. The factory eventually closed in 1966 following the retirement of its owner.

Lougher's factory in Norbury Road where some of the original buildings can still be seen.

Two internal views of the factory in the 1920s.

The reputation of our Preserve
Pickles and Sauces has been b
up and maintained over a peri
of 90 years. Today CHIVERS is
household word throughout t
Principality. Our Jams and Ma
malades enjoy a reputation
purity and quality which was t
aim of the founder and has be
the pride of an unbroken line
Chivers.

Chivers

**S. CHIVERS & CO. LTD.
ELY, CARDIFF**

SECTION OF JAM DEPARTMENT   ALSO MANUFACTURERS OF PICKLES AND S

A Chivers advertisement, 1954.

THE CHIVERS FAMILY originally came from Burford in the Cotswolds, and then moved to Cinderford in the Forest of Dean. Two sons of this family moved west, one to Ammanford and one, J. Chivers, to Pontypridd where he started a chemical works. He had two sons, one of whom was Samuel Chivers (b. 1843), who was educated at a small boarding school in Charles Street, Cardiff. The sons, after leaving, returned to work for their father, but Samuel eventually left the business, which was not big enough to keep the three families, and set up a pickle factory at East Canal Wharf in 1894 at the age of 30. He lived at 24 Dumfries Place. The factory was soon too small, so a move was made to Upper Grange in 1897. This factory was sold to Freeman's Cigars in 1900 when Chivers moved again to Ely. This factory cost £5,000 to build in 1900 and employed up to 100 people, many of whom were women. Women worked from 8 a.m. to 5 p.m. and the men from 6.30 a.m. to 5 p.m. Wages were 15s per week for women and £2 for men. In 1910-12 the Wage Council introduced a minimum wage, which meant that the female staff 'caught up' with the men a little; wages then rising to £1. 5s for women and £2. 10s for men. There was a strike for one week in the 1920s, which it is thought was about the establishment of a union in the factory.

In the early days at Ely, goods were transported to Cardiff, Barry and Penarth by four horse-drawn drays. The rest of the goods went by rail from Ely station. At the beginning of the First World War three of the horses were requisitioned by the Army leaving the firm with only the oldest, weakest horse. It was discovered afterwards that they need only have given one of the horses!

Chivers' staff around 1900.

In its heyday, the firm brewed 200,000 gallons of vinegar a year. Chivers was also famous for jam with most of the fruit coming by rail from Evesham. During the Second World War when sugar was rationed the government only allocated enough to correspond with the amount of fruit available.

The Chivers were prominent Methodists and Liberals, both Samuel and his son Ernest. After Ernest, Charles Padfield became Managing Director (1944-1956) and he was followed by Mr Samuel Chivers of Penarth (1956-1966) and Mr John Chivers (1966-1976). The firm was sold in 1977 to Fieldsman Preserves and was finally closed in October 1980.

Chivers' factory, 1920.

Chivers' drivers and their lorries outside the factory in the early 1950s. In 1963, Chivers was still employing 90 people (67 of whom were women); the staff numbers increased each year prior to Christmas and summer. Of the total workforce, 54 were from Ely.

The pickling plant in Spring 1980 – the year of the factory's closure. The buildings are still visible from the main road and the name S. Chivers (top left of above photograph) remains, some 16 years after the ending of production here.

View towards Caerau Lane/Caerau Road junction from Cowbridge Road West showing the Western Welsh offices in the foreground. The Western Welsh Omnibus Co. Ltd was registered in 1929 after various amalgamations over a number of years. Some names that came under their umbrella were the firms of Lewis, Barrett, James and Cridland. The Western Welsh fleet covered the whole of South Wales and as far west and north as Newquay and Builth Wells. At the main depot in Penarth Road, Cardiff, facilities were very limited and consequently repairs were carried out at outlying depots already established by some of the companies absorbed by the Western Welsh organisation. The establishment of a large and up-to-date central works where the whole fleet could be overhauled was obviously demanded and so the site at Ely was acquired and opened in early 1931. The main shop was built 295 yards long by 120 yards wide with stores, paint shop, coachbuilders, fitters and machine shops flanking it on one side.

Bus undergoing an overhaul at the new Western Welsh workshops in 1931.

Two views of the Western Welsh workshops, early 1931. It was not until 1965 that the office block was opened, when the staff moved from Central Station to the new building. In early 1981 all the workshops were closed in Ely and the work transferred to Chepstow. One of the last uses of the workshop was for the staging of the Ely Opera in 1984 as part of the Ely Festival. The site was later completely demolished and the Safeway supermarket, was built on the site.

Six

At Prayer, Play and War

THE NONCONFORMIST MOVEMENT

The first Methodist chapel in Ely was a barn in Mill Road given in 1806 by Thomas Morgan who owned a smallholding nearby. The railway brought an increase in Ely's population and the first chapel was replaced by a larger building; the official opening took place on 10 February 1858 with all the services in Welsh.

By 1867 six or seven English speakers were meeting in the house next to the chapel. The influx of English people to Ely saw the Welsh language declining so in 1874 a controversial decision was taken to conduct the Sunday school in English and by 1879 the chapel was completely English-speaking. This caused much protest with 'Thomas Griffiths and his wife preferring to walk from Ely to the Welsh chapel in Union Street when the Ely chapel became anglicised'. The new chapel, opened in 1911 on the corner of Cowbridge Road West and Colin Way (formerly Paget Street), had seating for 700 and was built by George Beames of Whitchurch at a cost of £2,894 10s 0d.

The laying of the foundation stone for Ely Methodist church on Cowbridge Road West, 11 November 1910. In the middle distance can be seen Palmer's greenhouses; the house on the left fronted onto Cowbridge Road and it was used as a shop for the market garden's produce — it is now a Chinese take-away. Beyond the greenhouses, on the left, can be seen St David's church hall and, on the right, Ely Council School, both in Clarke Street. The chimneys behind the school belong to Ely Paper Mills.

Revd Gethin Howell, with the founding members of Archer Road Baptist church.

In 1981 Mrs Crumpton described how the church began: 'It was built 53 years ago after a great tussle with the Baptist Union. We already had the ground given to us by the council. Our church started in the home of Mr and Mrs Evans, 11 Glyndwr Road, Ely. It was packed to capacity every evening. Our two husbands went every Sunday morning to get the room ready for the services, then Sunday school in the afternoon with tiny tots in the kitchen. Also, there were classes in other houses. Several conversions took place with meetings in the week: Tuesday – Christian endeavour, Wednesday – sisterhood and Thursday – prayer meeting. The baptists at Gabalfa loaned chairs and hymn books and Mr Simmons donated an organ. At the end of each Sunday it all had to be packed away in the back bedroom. The Baptist Union visited, saw how packed we were and finally agreed to a church being built'. This opened on 13 September 1928.

Ely Wesleyan Band of Hope, c. 1905.

St David's women's group at the vicarage, c. 1920. The vicar is Revd Francis. The vicarage is now the Welcare hostel run by the Llandaff diocesan board of social responsibility and is situated on Cowbridge Road West next to the new St David's vicarage. In 1871 a new church parish had been created and until 1903 vestry meetings for both St Mary's and St David's (consecrated on 23 November 1871) were held in Caerau. The vicar, Revd G.G. Williams, recorded at his first vestry meeting in 1894 that four people were present, and the annual offertory for both churches amounted to £5 6s 9d with the expenditure being £24 2s 8d. The churchwarden Mr J.H. Brain, who lived at 'Highmead' generously paid the shortfall! By 1919 no vestry meetings were held at St Mary's indicating the growing popularity and convenience of St David's.

Easter Monday, 1903. Gladys Davies (right) and Flossie Davies at the wedding of Mr and Mrs William Richard Thorne. The photograph was taken at the back of E. Davies' grocer's shop on the corner of Mill Road.

The wedding of Lilian and Wybert Arthur Cluett on 26 June 1915 which took place in Llandaff Cathedral. Both these photograph was taken at the rear of 564 Cowbridge Road East.

The bouquet contained roses and sweetpeas. At the time of their marriage Mrs Cluett was in service earning 6s a week but had to pay back 2s towards the cost of her uniform. Mr Cluett was a milkman delivering twice a day and earning 5s a week.

The wedding of Hannah ('Nan') Rees and Mr Oliver taken in the dairy next-door to 507 Cowbridge Road East.

The wedding of George Sutton and Olive Billinghurst, Redhouse Road, 1940.

Addison Crescent street party to celebrate the Festival of Britain in 1951. The street was named after the Addison Act of 1919 which enabled the provision of council housing.

Coronation celebrations outside Pethybridge Hall, Pethybridge Road on 16 June 1953.

Crosswells Brewery football team playing away at Lydney, 1950.

Council-run sports and recreation facilities could be found at the racecourse site (Trelai Park) and Archer Road (North Ely) but there were also a number run by staff welfare associations. Thomas Owen's paper mill sports ground was in Mill Road; the Co-operative Society's Wheatsheaf Club was off Amroth Road (it was gutted by fire on 3 March 1968 and Bromley Drive was later built on this site); towards the end of Cwrt-yr-Ala Road could be found Spiller's cricket ground and the university had its sports ground and pavilion in the open fields behind Caerau Lane School, later to be bisected by the Heol Trelai extension.

Ely Bowling Club, 1936.

Ely Paper Mill ladies' swimming team which won the Cardiff Ladies Squadron race in 1934 beating John Currans Ltd in the final round. Mr Armstead, the manager of the paper mill, is in the middle standing next to Emily Winter, who was twice a Welsh amateur swimming champion.

Pageant at Windsor Clive Junior School, 1934.

Sunday school opera at the United Reformed church, Grand Avenue, 1948. The church's foundation stone was laid on 7 September 1926 and the Sunday school opened with 457 children! A hall was purchased in 1947 at a cost of £500 and re-erected at a cost of £1,600. In the 1980s, the hall burnt down and the church sold the land for a new family centre. The original church was demolished and a new multi-purpose church was opened in the 1990s.

Cast of the Church of the Resurrection passion play, 19 March 1937. The Revd Bolt is the vicar front left with the Revd Redvers Evans front right.

Ely Racketeers outside Glan Ely Hall, Church of the Resurrection, in 1928. The Racketeers were formed to raise money for charity by giving concerts.

Chivers' workers outing, *c.* 1925.

Riverside Terrace residents leaving The White Lion pub on a day trip to Ledbury, early 1930s.

Sisterhood outing from Ely Methodist church, early 1930s. The photograph was taken in Mill Road showing the stables in the background.

Advertisement for the 1936 Welsh Grand National which was being run on the Cardiff racecourse in Ely.

CARDIFF RACES

Easter Monday & Tuesday
April 13th and 14th

WELSH GRAND NATIONAL
1936

FIRST RACE
2.30 p.m. EACH DAY.

A record entry and attractive programme ensure two good days sport.

Special trips running from all parts of South Wales

ELY RACECOURSE

In the *Cardiff Times* on 7 March 1862 the racing correspondent wrote: 'A word to the sportsmen of Cardiff. The attempts made to get up a steeplechase in 1861-62 failed miserably. They would be advised to reconsider flat racing'. However, by Easter 1864 the races were 'the most brilliant and successful ever held'. Trains from all over South Wales and the West of England brought spectators, trainers, horses and jockeys to Ely station, although in 1867 it was said 'the usual faint attempt at running trains between Cardiff and Ely every twenty minutes was also made, but with the usual customary inability to come to time'.

In 1895 the first Welsh Grand National was run at Ely. A large crowd broke down the entrance and the police had a hard job preventing people from getting in free. The following year the Welsh Grand National was won by the 1893 Liverpool Grand National winner, Cloister.

There was no racing during the First World War. It was started again in 1920, when the first prize in the Welsh Grand National was 460 sovereigns. In 1926 the local amateur rider, David Thomas of Cowbridge, riding his own horse, Miss Balscadden, won the race, beating the favourite, Postinao, by a head. Two years later Miss Balscadden won the race again. From 1934 onwards the National was dominated by one rider and one owner, Jack Fawcus and Mr J.V. Rank. Jack Fawcus won the race four times, but his first win in 1934 on Dream Ship was somewhat lucky. Really True started favourite and led at the last fence, but suddenly he swerved off the course and crashed into some hurdles. Dream Ship, left in the lead, won easily. Really True's bridle had broken as he came to the last fence. In 1936 the famous horse Golden Miller ran in the National, but could only finish third. Lacatoi won the race three times, in 1935, 1937 and 1939, the last National run in Ely.

Complimentary 'tickets' for entrance to the races. These were given out by the Cardiff Race Club to those people undertaking 'voluntary social work' in the Ely community.

The paddock at Ely Racecourse, 22 April 1924.

The grandstand at Ely Racecourse, 1898.

The destruction by fire of the two main stands in 1937 contributed to the end of racing in Ely. Within one hour of the alarm being raised, the stands were reduced to smouldering ruins. The land was owned by Cardiff Corporation and the buildings by Cardiff Race Club. There were suggestions that new stands could be built on the high ground below the wood, but a Cardiff City Council sub-committee recommended that the Race Club be allowed use of the course for a further two years only, with no assurances of the lease being renewed after this period.

On 27 April 1939 a horse called Grasshopper, ridden by Keith Piggott, won the last race held in Ely. A new grandstand catering for sports events on the racecourse was built after the Second World War. This remained until 1961 when it was demolished.

Main stands at Ely Racecourse. The buildings of Ely Hospital can be seen on the left with the Ely Paper Mills visible in the distance.

The parade of horses for the Welsh Grand National on Tuesday 22 April 1924. From left to right, the horses are Gem, Snipes Bridge, Mr Madcap and Bodyguard.

Ivor (left) and Jack Anthony, two brothers from the famous racing family after whom The Anthonys public house in Bishopston Road, Ely is named. Ivor Anthony trained three Welsh Grand National winners at Ely.

Mrs Greatrex wearing her father's colours at the rear of 70 Mill Road, *c.* 1900.

Ely stables, early 1940s. The foal was owned by Mrs Attwell who lived in Lansdowne Road. The main stables for Ely Racecourse were situated behind 'Great House' (later to become the British Legion club) on Cowbridge Road with an entrance from Mill Road.

Herbert Thompson School sports day on the racecourse, early 1950s. The grandstand in the background was built specially for sports events after the Second World War.

Victory celebrations in 1918 at the grandstand of Ely racecourse. Mr Edgar Edwards who lived in Highmead House organised and paid for the party. Each child was presented with a mug (see below) to mark the occasion.

A number of soldiers' graves from the First World War can be found in St Mary's churchyard: 23346 Private J. Murray, Welch Regt. 26th May 1919, aged 17; Private Harry Blick, 11th Welch Regt. who died in hospital at Salonika of malaria, Sept 26th 1916, aged 24 years; James Murray of Lord Strathcona's Horse, killed in France, Oct 9th 1918, aged 34 years.

After the Second World War, part of the Western Cemetery was dedicated as a military graveyard and a memorial cross can be seen at the Cowbridge Road/Michaelston Road corner.

The first British Legion committee in Ely, formed in 1943. The white building at the rear is the skittle alley of the old club. Those known in the photograph are, from left to right, front row: Bill Teague, Mrs Ball (stewardess), Ted Scuse, Mr Ball (steward) and Mr James. Middle row: Bill Goss, Mr Adams and L. Coleman. Back row: Mr Pengelley (left) and C. Jones. The British Legion remains a thriving Ely club and is now housed in a new building on the original site near The White Lion in Cowbridge Road West.

THE SECOND WORLD WAR AND ELY

In common with many other areas, detachments of the Home Guard were set up but the war effort also saw the building of a large military establishment in the middle of Ely. This establishment was to become known as RAF Llandaff. On 17 January 1939 proposals to sell 31 acres of land to the Air Ministry for the purpose of housing a balloon squadron to protect the city from aerial attack were discussed by the City Council (Cardiff was to be allocated Squadron No. 935 for this purpose). Although there was some initial objection, by August 1939 the depot was ready for action and capable of housing and servicing barrage-balloons in two large hangars on the site. These hangars survived long after the station was decommissioned with the site split up for the use of the Territorial Army and cadet forces. The barrage-balloons were taken to several sites throughout the area, including the racecourse fields, where they were flown to deter low-flying enemy aircraft. A factory in Llandaff North was set up to manufacture the balloons. Later, aircraft engines were also serviced at RAF Llandaff, which like the balloons, entered and left the depot by road, as there was no runway. Some of the ancillary buildings, such as the motor-transport garages, remain to this day but the major part of the site was cleared to make way for the Western Leisure Centre which opened in July 1978.

Anti-aircraft guns and an experimental rocket battery were also stationed on the racecourse fields as part of the air defence of the city. A rescue, repair and decontamination unit was also based at the racecourse. The main Air Raid Precautions (ARP) warden's post for Ely was Red House Farm, a local garage acted as an auxiliary fire station, and a depot and ambulance station was attached to Windsor Clive School.

Ely Brewery Home Guard No. 1 Platoon, 22nd Glam. (Cardiff) Battalion. An ARP warden's station was situated next to Davies' Café (formerly the Candle King shop) in Mill Road.

VE day street party in Caerau Square, 1945. Revd Redvers Evans is seated, front right.

Victory over Japan (VJ) celebrations in 1945 outside the recreation room in the building at the top of Archer Road. The site is now used as a play centre run by Cardiff County Council.

VJ celebration in Camrose Road, 1945.

Wartime photograph taken inside one of the hangars. Much of the work undertaken at RAF Llandaff was by women.

Part of the barrage-balloon hangars looking towards the Wenvoe transmitter mast, 1960s.

Motor-transport offices and parade ground of the barrage-balloon site. This photograph was taken in 1962 when the site was being run by the Territorial Army. The roof of the Church of the Resurrection can be clearly seen on the horizon. Small workshops operated by Cardiff County Council for Community Enterprise occupy part of the site today.

Territorial Army site on 7 June 1968, taken from the entrance into Caerau Lane.

The workmen who built the Regent Cinema in Mill Road, 1927.

The staff of the Regent Cinema which opened to the public on 25 October 1927. The cinema was one of a chain owned by the Splott (Cardiff) Company who claimed to be the largest entertainers of the public in Cardiff. On its first bill Ivor Novello and Mable Poulton starred in *The Constant Nymph*. Within a week the cinema was playing Murnau's classic silent movie *Sunrise* with Janet Gaynor and George O'Brien. The Regent closed in late 1968 and was converted into a bingo hall. Following the opening of purpose-built bingo halls in the 1990s the Regent Bingo Hall closed in 1995. Following a recent fire the Regent has now been demolished.

The Regent Cinema in 1961.

The Avenue Cinema was built on Cowbridge Road West next to the junction with Hill Snook Road. It opened to the public at 4.30 p.m. on Monday, 12 February 1940. An article accompanying the opening stated 'a modern architectural colossus has arisen in Ely' and went on to explain that 'decorations which are finished in a peach pink exude a pleasant warm softness which the psychologists will probably tell you will create just the right atmosphere for that mental relaxation which you seek in a cinema'. The first two films on the opening night were *Three Smart Girls Grow Up* with Deanna Durbin and *Secret Service of the Air* starring Ronald Reagan. This photograph was taken in 1957-8 when the two films playing were *Girl he left Behind* starring Natalie Wood and Bing Crosby's *Man on Fire*. The cinema closed in the early 1960s and is currently a Blockbuster video hire shop.

The usherettes and doorman of the Regent Cinema. Connie Derrick (left) remembers starting work there in 1943 at the age of 15 with seven other staff. Her day began at 7.30 a.m. by scrubbing eight rows of seats on each side for two hours, then other duties, going home for lunch and returning for matinée and evening performances finishing at 10.30 p.m. When she became cashier and the audience was seated she occasionally slipped over to St Clare's Hall to have a dance and return in time to tip the seats up!

Left: Miss Beatrice McCarthy in her cinema uniform. Right: A joint advertisement for both the Regent and Canton cinemas, 4 March 1936.

Seven

Communicating with a
wider world

From time immemorial Ely has been linked to the wider world; from its straddling of the ancient highway that crossed the River Ely at its lowest fording point (later the site of one of the first permanent bridges in the region). A turnpike and important coaching/posting highway, this road remained a strategic highway until the building of the M4. Although The Dusty Forge was a long-established inn it was not used by mail coaches as a regular stop. Some, however, could not pass this stretch of Cowbridge Road quickly enough. In an old Glamorgan house-book the owner wrote 'One of the places said to be frequented by the 'Evil Being' was a nook near The Dusty Forge Inn on the coach road to Cardiff. Whenever I passed that spot I closed my eyes, and buried my face in my hands, and kept my head well down until we had made our way over the great hill known as Tumble-down-Dick which was to me the place of great temptation'.

Strategic links of another kind were forged with the building of the South Wales Railway through Ely in the late 1840s, providing direct links between London and the West Wales ports of Neyland and Fishguard, and serving industrial South Wales. Engineered by Isambard Kingdom Brunel, this broad-gauge line was converted to standard gauge in 1872.

There were also direct sea links dating back to the Romano-British period with the villa having its own connection to the River Ely, giving direct access to the sea. This was a link that was indirectly restored towards the end of the last century and the beginning of this century with prominent ship-owners settling in the Ely area.

This century saw a re-emergence of road traffic attracting local enterprise, with the Worrell Brothers opening their first garage in the Ely area in 1922. Seven years later a consortium that was to become one of the largest bus operators, Western Welsh, began planning and building its depot. The last development of the trolley-bus also centred on Ely with trolley-buses running until 1970.

Ely also had a stake in a radically different mode of transport – aircraft – with flying on Ely racecourse. The connection with flying resumed during the Second World War with the maintenance of wartime barrage-balloons and aero-engines. Curiously an iron-framed building that had been used to manufacture balloons by the Welsh airship pioneer, Ernest Willows, was removed to Ely to serve as a concrete casting shed for the construction of houses.

Today, Ely is overshadowed by a modern form of communication – the Wenvoe television transmitter – and a major television studio (HTV) is based at Culverhouse Cross.

Cowbridge Road West, c. 1910, at what is now the junction with Vincent Road. Ely Hospital can clearly be seen on the left.

Ely Bridge, 1906. Both these photographs shows the state of the road before it was surfaced in 1911 when the bridge was rebuilt.

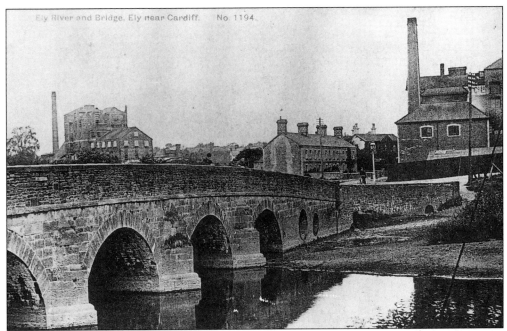

Ely River and Bridge, Ely near Cardiff. No. 1194.

Ely River and Bridge, 1900. Mr Ivor Harris recollected that about this time Patsey Regan owned Dennies Island – a bank of silt a few yards away from the bridge and surrounded by water. Mr Regan's horse grazed on the island but often was rescued during flooding. But no experience of this nature could persuade him from discontinuing to graze his pony there. The island can just be seen on the right-hand side of the photograph.

Ely Bridge, 1940.

Workmen building the new bridge in 1910. This view is looking towards Ely Paper Mill. The top of the railway bridge can be seen above the railway goods vans.

Ely Bridge, c. 1920. The top right-hand corner shows that the fields for the Ely estate have not yet been built upon. Until the opening of the M4 this road through Ely remained the main route to Swansea and all places in West Wales.

Cowbridge Road West and Amroth Road junction in 1960. At this time these was no need for traffic lights. Situated behind this row of shops was the Children's Ear, Nose and Throat Hospital.

Cowbridge Road West, 2 April 1970. The traffic delays were caused by structural work on Ely Bridge. The white house, originally known as 'Great House', and displaying the Ely ales advertisements was demolished to make way for the building of the new British Legion club.

Worrell's Garage, 1927. The garage stood opposite St David's church on Cowbridge Road West. Offices have now been built on the site.

These photographs were taken at the time of King George V's Silver Jubilee in 1935. Crossway's Garage was built in 1927 on Cowbridge Road West between Caerau Lane and St Francis' church opposite the West End Club. The site is now an Esso garage.

Ely Bridge, 1969, showing the structural work taking place. The trolley-buses were still running to Ely at this time.

Trolley-bus at the junction of Grand Avenue and Heol Muston (formerly Phyllis Crescent), c. 1968. In 1939, Cardiff Corporation decided to convert its ageing tramway network to a trolley-bus operation. With the trolley-buses came an experimental method of fare collections which involved the use of fareboxes to collect fares from passengers as they boarded. In accordance with the council's policy to provide the city workers with cheap transport a flat fare of 1d was charged for any journey. Around 1950, double-decker trolley-buses became available and although railed electric traction had come to an end in Cardiff, trolley-buses continued to flourish and on delivery of the final thirteen double-deckers in 1955, the system was extended to Ely. By the late 1960s, trolley-buses in Cardiff were coming to the end of their usefulness and a trolley-bus conversion programme took place. This was completed on 3 December 1969 although new Daimler Fleetline motor-buses had already been operating alongside the trolley-buses for some months. Trolley-buses continued to operate 'enthusiasts' specials' until 11 January 1970, when a specially decorated bus finally ran into Roath depot, marking the end of electric traction in South Wales.

Flower's Garage, 1960s. The garage was just west of the Heol Trelai/Cowbridge Road West junction. Behind the garage the land was still fields and allotments. The garage has now become an American discount golf shop.

Trolley-bus at Christmas, c. 1968, at the junction of Green Farm Road and Cowbridge Road West.

Mr Edgar Edwards of Highmead House [see pages 22-23], a Cardiff ship-owner in the 1920s. E. Edwards & Sons Ltd advertised itself as 'steamship owners and brokers, coal contractors'. They were based at Pier Head Chambers in Cardiff and also had an office in London. They were the managers of Western Counties Shipping Co. Ltd, with responsibility for 24 ships including one called *Highmead*.

The *Lowmoor*, one of the ships of E. Edwards & Sons Ltd.

Ely station staff, 1925. Included in the photograph are: Mr Heaven (station-master), Bill Smith (chief ticket collector), Mr Doel (goods clerk), Mr Green and Evan Sergeant (platform porters), Mr Lightfoot and Bert Smith (goods porters), Miss Cotterell (booking clerk) and Charlie Martin (goods clerk). The South Wales Railway opened on 18 June 1850, and the Ely station on Monday, 2 September 1850. The Penarth, Harbour Dock and Railway (which crosses over Cowbridge Road East by the Paper Mill) opened on 1 July 1859. Although for many years only a goods station served Ely from this line it has been recently opened to passenger traffic and provides the nearest station (Waungron Park) to Ely.

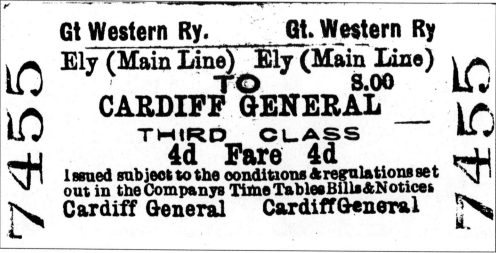

Ely station ticket issued on 10 June 1935 when the fare from Ely to Cardiff Central was 4d.

A coal train heading towards Barry passing the Drope junction signal box. The line to Peterston-super-Ely is on the left. The Barry railway main line ran along the western edge of Ely with its most famous feature to Ely people being the Drope viaduct which was built in the 1890s. The line closed in the 1960s and the Culverhouse Cross – M4 link now runs along part of the old railway route.

A Great Western 2-8-0 T leads a mixed load of open wagons through Ely station, late 1960s. The station-house can be seen to the right with the brewery in the background.

A Great Western 2-8-0 T on a loaded coal train passing the Ely signal box in front of Crosswells brewery. The wagons on the left were for the use of local coal merchants such as Charles W. Williams.

COAL COAL

For GOOD Coal go to—

Charles W. Williams & Son

ESTABLISHED 1879.

Coal and Coke Merchants and Haulage Contractors

ELY STATION

Special Quotations for Large Quantities.
Prices on Application.

Orders and Enquiries to—   *Telephone :* 112 *LLANDAFF.*

Only Address—8 ST. FAGANS ROAD, ELY

Depots—ELY STATION and FAIRWATER SIDINGS

This advertisement was placed in various publications in the 1930s.

A Great Western Railway Hall class locomotive enters Ely main line station on an up Swansea – Bristol train. The station was simply called Ely originally but in 1923 the Great Western Railway took over the Taff Vale Railway and as that company also had a goods depot named Ely (on the line from Penarth Curve to Radyr) it left the GWR with two Ely stations – one on the main line (passenger and goods) and the ex-TVR one (goods only). To differentiate between the two the words 'main line' and 'Fairwater Road' respectively were added on 1 July 1924.

A group of Ely schoolboys from Herbert Thompson School about to leave Ely station to go to the Festival of Britain in London, 1951. The station was closed for passengers on 10 September 1962 and for goods traffic on 5 August 1963.

This photograph was taken on 22 September 1911 and shows the *Mercury* taking off from Ely Racecourse with the Paper Mill in the background. The *Western Mail* reported that 'History was made at Ely near Cardiff on Saturday and it is difficult to estimate the far-reaching significance of what took place. Mr H. Grindell-Matthews, the inventor of the aerophone, succeeded under almost the worst conditions possible in establishing communication by wireless telephony with an aeroplanist careering through the air, 700 feet high, in strong wind and rain, and at a speed equal to an express train. The most sanguine hopes of the experts on the ground were more than realised, and the inventor went away highly pleased. Mr B.C. Hucks the plucky young aviator who braved the elements under conditions the majority of flying men would have deemed too dangerous, is also very much elated at being the first airman to take part in wireless telephony. His fine Blackburn monoplane, the *Mercury*, acted splendidly in the tricky wind and when he descended with the telephone receivers still tied round his head he was given a very hearty cheer'.

The next day the pilot was back at the racecourse giving a flying display charging 1s to enter although entrance was 3d for 'boys in the uniforms of the church lads' brigade and boy scouts'. Ely Racecourse saw other historic moments in aviation history. It was reported on 14 October 1919 that a 'large company gathered at Ely racecourse to witness the navigation of the Cardiff-London -Paris aviation (airmail) service of Messrs S. Instone and Co.'. A letter was handed to the pilot, Lieut. Barnard, from the Cardiff Chamber of Commerce to the Paris Chamber of Commerce. The plane took off and 'rose beautifully against the wind and after circling Sweldon Farm… a couple of times and doing a few daring stunts the pilot and his mechanic were away on their long trip'.

Two months previously Ely had been offered a grand flying week with passenger flights at £1 1s 0d return. The *Western Mail* reporter was exuberant after taking a flight and stated that 'an interesting feature of the navigation was the filming of the first flight by the Gaumont Film Company'.

In the early 1930s flying was still taking place at the racecourse with Pat O'Hara making a 1,000 foot parachute drop from the airliner *Prince Henry* as well as walking the wings in mid-air displays. The cost of the flights had decreased considerably since 1919 and could now be obtained from 5s to 10s 6d.

JOY FLYING AT CARDIFF.

GRAND FLYING WEEK AT ELY RACECOURSE,

COMMENCING SATURDAY, AUGUST 7th.

PASSENGER FLIGHTS in Latest Type Two - passenger AVRO AEROPLANES,

From £1 1s. 0d.

Flying Daily from Eleven a.m. to Dusk. Frequent tram service to Canton terminus.

CROSS-COUNTRY FLIGHTS undertaken at Short Notice on application to A. R. VAN DEN BURGH (late Lieut.), at the Flying Ground.   a3073

Advertisement for joy-flying at Ely, 6 August 1920.

FOR ONE WEEK ONLY.

Imperial Airways AIR LINER " Prince Henry"
At ELY RACECOURSE, MONDAY, April 27,
Till SUNDAY, May 3 (inclusive).

FLYING NOON TILL DUSK.————SUNDAY 10 a.m. TILL DUSK.
Passenger Flights 10/6, 7/6, 5/-. Special Flights in Avro 10/-.

WALKING THE WINGS IN MID-AIR, to be followed by PARACHUTE DESCENTS at 6.30 p.m. (weather permitting)
On WEDNESDAY, SATURDAY, & SUNDAY.
Admission 6d. Children 3d. Car Park 1/-.

Advert for Imperial Airways at Ely Racecourse, 27 April 1931.

'Sunday at Culver', 1950s, with some of the 'gallery' in the background. This plus the following two photographs illustrate the changes that Ely continues to experience. In the 1950s the Culverhouse Cross roundabout was surrounded by countryside, and Ely people congregated there to watch the traffic and meet friends. Forty years later people still meet at the same venue but now the area is an out-of-town shopping complex with Tescos, Marks and Spencers and the Vale Gate Retail Park. A 1996 survey found Culverhouse Cross to be the fourth most popular centre for shoppers in South Wales with 98 per cent of people arriving by car.

This aerial photograph was taken in the mid-1970s. The main road can clearly be seen running through the whole of Ely towards Cardiff. The barrage-balloon site has been cleared but the Western Leisure Centre has not yet been built nor has the Ely link road. Sweldon Farm, right foreground behind Mary Immaculate Roman Catholic School, awaits demolition for housing.

This aerial photograph taken on 27 October 1982 highlights the ever-changing face of Ely. In 1996 the route from Cardiff docks to the M4, the out-of-town shopping centre and the Copthorne Hotel are thriving, HTV have studios on the site and the house by the roundabout has been demolished to make way for the Wyndham car sales showroom. Despite the protests of residents in Brooklands Terrace there are plans to build another major retail development on the site. As physical developments continue rapidly in and around Ely it is the individual experiences of Ely people that remains paramount and it has been the aim of this book to illustrate some of their achievements.

Acknowledgements

Plans for an Ely Old and New exhibition began in 1978 with the copying of old photographs belonging to Ely residents and those with Ely connections. The aim was to enhance the image of Ely by looking at the area's past and proving there was a history of which to be proud. The work was undertaken by the staff at the Ely Community Shop (Barnardos) as a small part of their community work initiative in the area. Without Barnardos' commitment to Ely, neither the exhibition or this book would have been possible. By 1985, over 1,100 photographs had been copied and the first of many showings of the exhibition was held at Trelai Youth Centre.

Particular thanks are due to: Revd Bob Morgan for writing the Foreword and endorsing the book; Martin Roberts who copied all the photographs for the exhibition and worked as photographer in residence at the Community Shop for over ten years; David Harding who designed the original exhibition; Colleagues in Ely Community Education who supported the work over the years: John Moore, Dorothy Stickler, Barry Doughty, Karol Knill, Alun Michael, John Winslade and John Rose; The Social Work Department of University College, Cardiff, who supplied numerous students over the years; Volunteers on the Ely Archive Project, Community Programme Agency (MSC) administered by Cardiff City Council, 1986-88, in particular project leaders, Gareth Morris and Kathryn Jones and all the Ely residents who supported the project; Philip Riden of the Extra-Mural Department of University College, Cardiff; Everyone connected with the Ely History Group with particular thanks to Harry Griffiths; Colleagues in Barnardos: Pauline Leeson, Ruth Stanford, Karen Lewis and Phyllis Watters, as well as, Shirley Collins in Ely Citizens Advice Bureau; Siân, Jude, Kathryn, Bethan, Naomi and Ruth. We trust that this book is of interest to readers far beyond the boundaries of Ely, but, to all Ely residents, we hope that this work does justice to your community.

Finally our thanks to all those people who have shared their photographs with us over the past eighteen years: Aerofilms Ltd; Mr Ainsbury; Air Photo Unit; Mr Baker; Mr Ballard; Bob Barrett; Bass Wales and West; Mr & Mrs Batty; Mr Beck; Enid Best; Mr & Mrs Biss; Mr Blackmore; Arthur Blannin; Revd & Mrs Bolt; Glyn Bowen; Garry and Elaine Brace; Tina Brain; Mrs Brooks; Mr Budd; Mrs Burton; Mr Busby; Mrs Casey; Derek Chaplin; Percy Charles; Mrs Chichester; Mr Chivers; Chivers pickle factory; Mrs Clowes; Mr & Mrs Cluett; Mrs Colliers; Mr Cooke; Mrs Criddle; Fred Criddle; Alma Cridland; Mrs Crumpton; Mrs M. Cumner; Mr Davies; Herbie Dawe; Mrs Connie Derrick; Mrs Dickens; Mr Dodd; Mrs Dodds; Violet Eddy; Mr & Mrs Edwards; Ely British Legion Club; Mrs Efiem; Mrs V. Elliott; Mrs Ellis; Mrs Emerson; Mrs Evans; Revd Mary Evans; Marion Florence; Miss M. Foot; Anne Gardner; Mr George; Mr Gower; Mrs Griffiths; Mr F.L. Guinee; Bruce Gully; Revd John Guy; Douglas Haig Memorial Homes; Nell & Viv Halbert; Mr Hall; B.M. Ham; Peggy Hamling; Doug Harris; Arthur W. Harrison; Jim Hathaway; Mrs Hayward; Mrs Hill; Mr Hitchman; Jim Holloway; Reg Howard; Graham Horwood; Mrs Howell; Jill James; Roy James; Mrs James; Mr James; C. Jarvis; Chris Jenkins; Miss G. Jenkins; Colin Jones (Fred J. Jones Collection); Huw Jones Photography; Karen Jones; Ken & Doreen Jones; Mr Jones; Mrs M. Jones; Mrs King; Michael Klamm; John Loosemore; Mrs Mansfield; Bernice Mawn; Mr & Mrs McElveen; Mr Millward; Mrs Millward; Dorothy Morgan; Eric Mountford; National Museum of Wales; Mrs Newman; Mr & Mrs Nicholls; Mr Nowells; Mrs O'Grady; Sandra & Roger Palmer; G. Parker; Mrs Parker; Mrs Parnell; Mrs Pengilly; Mrs Phillips; Liz Pitman; David Plank, Planning Department, Cardiff County Council; Ken Poole; Myra Roberts; Mrs Russell; Mrs Rutter; W. Salter; Mr Saunders; Mrs Scott; Mrs G.M. Sheehan; Mr Smith; Mrs Smith; Terence Soames Ltd; Mr Southall; Mr Spriggs; Staff of Ely and Central Library; Mr & Mrs Stork; Mr Stradling; Bill Streubig; Ernie Strong; Mrs Strong; V. Sully; Mr C. Taylor; Miss Thoburn; Dave Thomas; Mr Thorne; Mrs Tomkins; Mrs Underdown; Mrs Vaggers; Glyn Waite; Mr Walker; Kath Walsh; Welsh Folk Museum; Welsh Industrial and Maritime Museum; Western Mail & Echo Ltd; Winnie Whitcomb; Barry Whittaker; Wiggins Teape (now Arjo Wiggins); Mrs Williams; Harriet Wilson; Fred Winter; Miss Woodman; Mr & Mrs Woolven; Mr J. Worrell.